Additional praise for *Making the News:*

"Salzman provides a terrific guide for attracting publicity
and working with the media. It should be useful to
students and professionals."

Susan Jacobson
University of Florida

"A great guide for community organizers, whether
they have $10 or $10,000 to spend on media."

Kate Reinisch
Director of Public Affairs,
Planned Parenthood of the Rocky Mountains

"I wish Jason Salzman would stop giving away our secrets."

Dick Kreck
Columnist, *Denver Post*

"An extremely useful and informative book that provides
everything an activist needs to know for communicating
effectively through the media."

David Cortright
President, Fourth Freedom Forum

"The best book available for learning how to define and
deliver messages that make news—and a difference."

Bill Walker
California Director,
Environmental Working Group

MAKING THE NEWS

MAKING THE NEWS

A Guide for Nonprofits
and Activists

JASON SALZMAN

Westview Press
A Member of the Perseus Books Group

Copyright © 1998 by Westview Press, A Member of the Perseus Books Group

Published in 1998 in the United States of America by Westview Press, 5500 Central Avenue, Boulder, Colorado 80301-2877, and in the United Kingdom by Westview Press, 12 Hid's Copse Road, Cumnor Hill, Oxford OX2 9JJ

Library of Congress Cataloging-in-Publication Data
Salzman, Jason.
   Making the news : a guide for nonprofits and activists / Jason
Salzman
      p.   cm.
   Includes bibliographical references and index.
   ISBN 0-8133-6898-7
   1. Publicity—United States.   2. Fund raising—United States.
3. Public relations—United States—Endowments.   4. Public
relations—United States—Social service.   5. Nonprofit
organizations—United States—Finance.   6. Endowments—United
States—Management.   7. Promotion of special events.   8. Mass media—
United States—Social aspects.   9. Mass media and social service—
United States.   I. Title.
HM263.S247   1998
659'.0973—dc21   98-9517
                                                                                 CIP

The paper used in this publication meets the requirements of the American National Standard for Permanence of Paper for Printed Library Materials Z39.48-1984.

10   9   8   7   6   5

Contents

Acknowledgments

IF YOU ARE A COMMUNITY ORGANIZER or nonprofit professional, this book is dedicated to you. You probably deserve more recognition than you get. But here's the catch: Now that you've got a media book dedicated to you, you are obliged to make media relations more of a priority in your work. Get the word out. It's worth the effort.

I'd also like to dedicate *Making the News* to my wife, Anne, and my parents, Manny and Joanne. (I realize I'm dedicating the book to a lot of people, but—like getting media attention—I say take the opportunity when you have it.) Anne directed her general intelligence and humor toward this project; her extensive editing help was invaluable. My mom has one of the most important qualities of a great activist: She never expects to lose. And my dad, who often expects to lose, is nonetheless brilliant at thinking of new ways to succeed. My parents are also media savvy. For example, even though they're both completely over the edge, they can—at the exact right moment in an interview—sound completely reasonable. This wins over reporters every time.

A first edition of this book, titled *Let the World Know: Make Your Cause News*, was published by Rocky Mountain Media Watch, a Denver-based nonprofit organization that I cofounded to challenge the news media, particularly local TV news, to be fair and balanced in reporting what's happening in our community. My colleagues and I believe that if journalists are going to do a good job, they need to hear from citizens with substantive story ideas. This book aims to help citizens get their message out. Lots of people at Rocky Mountain Media Watch helped conceptualize the book, especially Paul Klite, who's been a constant source of encouragement. He made wise comments on various drafts. Andy Bardwell, John Boak (who designed the front cover), Barb Donachy, Tory Read, and Kate Reinisch also helped get the book off the ground.

Leo Wiegman at Westview Press has been a source of rapid-response wisdom. Unlike many people, he believed in this book from the moment he heard about it. Until I met Leo and others at Westview—including Kristin Milavec, Adina Popescu, and Melanie Stafford—most of my experience with the book-publishing world consisted of rejection letters with an annoying good-bye such as "We wish you the best of luck in finding an appropriate publisher." I'm thankful Leo did not send me such a letter. I'm also lucky Diane Hess copyedited the manuscript so skillfully.

Thanks to all the journalists who let me interview them for this book. Not only did most journalists I called readily accept my request for an interview but they wanted to do it immediately—so as not to drag out the distraction from their work. Writing this book reminded me again how many committed, conscientious people work for news organizations. But it also brought to light the difficult conditions most journalists face at their jobs, particularly as staffs shrink and ownership of major news outlets is concentrated in the hands of a smaller and smaller number of large corporations.

Thanks to these nonprofit professionals and activists: Asonga Abeywickrema, David Akerson, Peter Andreas, Ed and Stephanie Benton, Nilak Butler, the Buttons, Twilly Cannon, Tom Clements, Beth Conover, David Culp, Scott Deming, the Forells, the Gerlachs, Claire Greensfelder, David and Peter Grinspoon, Don Hancock, Scott and Thakane Haase, Adam and Tracy Hollaway, Amy Hudson, Anna Jones, Jev Katz, David Lewis, Linus Lund, Lester and Ella Lurie, Bob McFarland, Jack Mento, Damon Moglen, LeRoy Moore, Darcy O'Brien, Jan Pilcher, Nelson and Martha Rangell, Tom Rauch, Tim Ream, Dave and Mary Reed, Dan

Reicher, Doug Richardson, Mike Roselle, Charnahmet and Dolanpete Salzman, Virginia Sarapura, Jacob Scherr, Mag and Ken Seaman, George Seidel, Ken Snyder, Mark Stevens, Susan Stroud, Ronnie Sunshine, Chet Tchozewski, Annie and Tim VanDusen, Bill Walker, Bill Walsh, Ralph and Julie Walsh, Harold Ward, Harvey Wasserman, Robin Weingarten, Valerie Wheeler, Mark Yanowitz, and Penelope Zeller.

Thanks to these folks whom I see in Telluride, Colorado, each year: Bill and Karen Adams, Art Goodtimes, Lee and Linnea Gillman, John Sir Jesse, Gary Lincoff, Jo and Carter Norris, Rita Rosenberg, Paul Stamets, and Andy Weil.

Finally, thanks to my son, Dylan, who was born a few months before I finished this book. Sometimes he tried to stop me from completing it—with middle-of-the-night wailing and midday whining—but most of the time he was quite agreeable, sleeping in his little chair next to my computer as I typed. Now that I've finished the book, he seldom sleeps.

Jason Salzman

MAKING THE NEWS

Introduction:
Let the World Know

WHY IS SO MUCH OF THE NEWS irrelevant? Why are we still watching the Big Stories about the beauty contest for cows, the pet lobster, meatloaf week in Florida, canine cocktails at the bookstore, or the attack of the giant tumbleweeds? And who hasn't heard enough "news" about guns, shootings, and bullets and more guns, shootings, and bullets?

It's easy to complain about mayhem and fluff in the news. And it's convenient to blame journalists for *not* covering issues and causes—stories that might help solve the problems our society faces.

But the truth is, every citizen shares the blame with the news media. We do not offer journalists enough opportunities—in the right packaging and at the right time—to cover causes and important issues.

Nonprofit organizations and activists are certainly part of the problem. On tight budgets, they often argue that trying to get media attention distracts them from doing the *real* work—managing programs, organizing, fund-raising, recruiting volunteers, and so on. So they are left struggling to save the world in the dim light of obscurity and wondering why more people don't value what they do. And worse, they never benefit from all the ways that getting media coverage can make their work easier.

Similarly, the "events" that political activists organize are often so boring that even the most sympathetic editors cannot include

1

Frequent demonstrations forced officials to erect this sign. Would you expect a rally here to make the news? You'll break into the news by being creative. Credit: Jason Salzman

them in today's competitive entertainment-oriented news "shows" or in the newspaper. For example, protesters in Nevada complain that they receive scant news coverage of their rallies at a former testing site for nuclear bombs near Las Vegas. Yet protests are so common there that the government has placed a permanent sign near the gate: DEMONSTRATORS ON ROAD-WAY. If you were an editor, how would you rate the news value of a rally near that sign? Admirable commitment to a cause, yes. Comedy, maybe. News, no.

Granted, there are lots of reasons to protest beyond getting news coverage. But if it's media attention you want—and it's clearly media attention you *need* in order to communicate to mass audiences—then you should learn how to be successful at attracting journalists to your cause. For many activists like me, this comes with a price: An effective media strategy requires—at least to some extent—a willingness to cater to the often warped priorities and short attention span of the news media.

The lack of news about nonprofit organizations explains, in part, why so many social problems remain unsolved. Adults in the United States watch an average of four hours or more of TV daily. With the attention of most people focused on their television sets, news coverage about a problem can be the first step toward a solution.

This book has all the information you need to publicize your cause in the local, national, and international news media. It's written specifically for activists, nonprofit groups, or any concerned citizen who doesn't have a big advertising budget but wants to get the word out.

I know from firsthand experience how busy the activists and staff at nonprofit organizations are. I understand how frustrating it is to pick up a book that's supposed to contain a few tips I can actually use in my day-to-day work only to find that it's been written by a theorist who's completely disconnected to my real-world needs.

This book, in contrast, was written for people who don't have time to read about how to change the world but have to figure out how to do it anyway. It's designed to be *used*—free of unnecessary jargon or theory and easy to understand. Its detailed index and table of contents allow you to access information quickly without having to read entire chapters, much less the entire book.

For example, if you're scheduled for a talk-radio show tomorrow, you can turn to Chapter 25 for tips on how to prepare. If you want information on how to publish a guest opinion in the newspaper, look at Chapter 20. Need to control a media crisis in a hurry? See Chapter 32. It's all concise and user-friendly.

What's in the Book?

Part 1 of *Making the News* explains how you can stage an event or stunt that will put an issue that concerns you in the news. It takes you through the entire process, starting with developing your message and ending with assessing your results. In between you'll find chapters on developing a simple message, determining what's newsworthy, choosing an effective time and location for your event, writing and distributing a news release, becoming a master interviewee, convincing reporters to attend your event, and more. Specific tips for publicizing art events and civil disobedience are also included.

Unique information in Chapter 4 explains how to create newsworthy images and symbols to communicate your message to a mass audience. With television more and more dominant in our society, words—especially written words—are weak and getting weaker as a tool for communicating. To reach most people, you have to package your message in an image or symbol. It can be fun and challenging to create newsworthy images, and Chapter 4 discusses how to do it, citing dozens of examples. In some cases, you'll be able to take an idea directly from this chapter and use it for your cause. In other cases, the ideas and examples will serve as models for you to adapt and to stimulate your own creativity.

There are, of course, times when an event is not appropriate or feasible. Part 2 details how to make news without staging an event. You'll discover how you can make news simply by calling a journalist on the phone or spending a few minutes in front of your computer. You'll find information on how to publish letters to the editor and guest opinions and how to persuade columnists and editorial page editors to write about your cause. Other chapters explain how to get booked on talk radio, how to pitch story ideas to reporters, how to lobby cartoonists and newspaper photographers for favorable coverage, and how to use community calendars. You'll also find specific tips on how to shine the media spotlight on nonprofit products and academic reports.

Part 3 explains what to do when disaster strikes and you are the *unwilling* object of a media frenzy. As more money flows to cause-oriented organizations, journalists are justifiably paying more attention to the nonprofit sector. Part 3 explains how any nonprofit organization can prepare for their unsolicited inquiries.

Part 4 offers ideas on how to develop long-term relationships with journalists, including advice on how to cultivate credibility as a news source. It outlines when to complain about media coverage and, if appropriate, how to complain. For those seriously angry about the news media, Chapter 36 offers a bare-bones approach to becoming an effective media watchdog.

Using the media is one tool, among many, to advance a cause. But eight inches of ink in the daily newspaper can be next to worthless if it is not linked to a strategy for winning your campaign. Although this handbook focuses on the media, Part 5 is included to help you begin thinking about how to link your "media work" with a larger strategy to achieve your goals.

Making the News ends with a list of resources to help you find names of journalists nationally and in your area. It also lists communications consultants, other media how-to handbooks, media literacy organizations, news media watchdog groups, and books about media and culture.

Inside-the-Media Insights from Journalists

Many people seem to think news is gathered and written by an amorphous power dispensing copy via the News God—who promotes greed and evil at the expense of real people and their interests. The truth is that news organizations are composed of people, a lot of whom want to talk to you and are trying to do a good job even as their employment is threatened by corporate mergers and changes in communications technologies.

Throughout this book, you'll find quotes from professional journalists. They offer their inside-the-media insights on how to put your cause on the airwaves and in print. Their comments, coupled with advice from activists, demystify the news and the news-gathering process.

It's not hard to make news, but not enough people try. That's why I wrote this book. During six years as a staff campaigner with media-savvy Greenpeace, I traveled around the United States and saw that community groups often use the media poorly or not at all. At the same time, I saw politicians and corporations fight each other to manipulate the news, knowing that whoever did the best "media work" could completely change how the public perceived the issues at hand.

These are high-stakes communications battles. For example, Rep. Newt Gingrich and his advisers recognized that it wasn't new ideas that were required to win a Republican majority in Congress but the ability to communicate old ones. Documents from Gingrich's political organization, quoted in the *New York Times*, reveal the belief that changes in U.S. politics required "fundamentally and essentially a COMMUNICATIONS PLAN."[1]

It's time for activists and nonprofit groups to fight back and harness the power of the news media. To succeed, they need to make a sustained commitment to their communications programs, dedicating scarce money and staff time *over the long haul*. It's easy enough to break into the news media once, but it's the repeated media hits—plus ongoing communications efforts— that will change the direction of our society.

Part One

How to Stage
a Media Event

Media events are the source of much of the "news," particularly political news, that lands on the doorstep or spills out of the TV. If you see the president on TV, you're probably looking at coverage of a media event planned and staged by the president's staff. They know that images and symbols on TV overpower words (and, often, deeds) as a vehicle of communication to mass audiences.

You don't need to have a multimillion-dollar budget to pull off a winning media event. All you have to do is understand basic information about how the news media work and know what resources you have (staff, volunteers, cash, props). Then you need to translate information about your cause into a language and form that is easy for the media to report to their audiences.

If you appreciate street theater, drama, and homespun art—like I do—you'll like executing media events. Organizing one is much like directing a play with props and dialogue. Similarly, if you like to poke fun at people, you'll likely stage effective media events; teasing requires the same natural inclination toward conflict and fun that an activist uses when designing a media stunt.

Staging an event to project your message is essential. Here's why: The news media, particularly television, rarely cover isolated opinions, ideas, or abstract views. Ideas, in the simple and image-dominated language of the media, are generally considered boring (and hence not newsworthy). But with some creativity, you can transform an idea or an opinion about a cause into an event that lends itself to media coverage.

Part 1 of this book is a guide to staging a media event. The chapters in Part 1 also describe how to make events such as civil disobedience, art shows, or performances newsworthy.

1

Develop
a Simple Message

YOUR FIRST TASK IN CREATING A MEDIA EVENT—or in
preparing to interact with journalists under any circumstance—is
to identify one simple message that you want to communicate. It
should summarize the essential information you want to convey.
Your message should be contained in one phrase; following are
some examples of messages for the news media:

> The incinerator will cause cancer.
> Don't tear down the old Sand Inn.
> Gov. Idlebrain does not support education.
> Put 100 more police officers on the streets.
> Stop hunting whales.
> Use cloth grocery sacks.
> Don't drink and drive.
> Vote yes on amendment 1.

Once you've clarified your message, you should create a couple of sound bites to communicate it to journalists. A sound bite
is a quotable statement supporting your message. And depending on the length of interviews you expect to have, you should
develop up to a half-dozen simple points to support your mes-

sage—each with one or more sound bites. (See Chapter 11, "Become a Master Interviewee.")

As Thoreau wrote, simplify, simplify, simplify. Journalists—television journalists, in particular—rarely confuse their audience with complex information, which might prompt some lazy people to change the channel. For this reason, the script of a newscast is generally written with the assumption that viewers comprehend at the sixth-grade level. To fit into this format, your message needs to be simple, clear, and easily understood.

As you develop your simple message for an event, be clear about what you want to accomplish. Maybe you want to awaken the public by sending frightening news. Maybe you want your community to know that the mayor is ignoring crimes in your neighborhood. Or maybe you want to draw attention to a piece of legislation addressing the problem.

Most politicians use polling data to decide what simple message they want to communicate. Then they develop images, supporting points, and sound bites to relay the message to the public. For example, according to Mark Hertsgaard in *On Bended Knee*, polling data showed that President Ronald Reagan's "negatives" were that people thought (1) he didn't care about education and (2) he might start a war. So his communications specialists arranged for Reagan to give speeches at universities and schools around the country, thereby associating him with positive educational images. His aides also advised against allowing him to be photographed with military weaponry, so that people would not associate him with war. (For more on this and other amazing tales of the Reagan public relations machine, read *On Bended Knee*. See also Chapter 44, "Further Reading on Media and Culture.")

Similarly, some activists working on an unpopular issue develop messages related to the *least* unpopular aspects of the issue. For example, because there is not much support in the United States for fewer prisons or the rehabilitation of prisoners instead of incarceration, a group of activists calling for prison reform decided they would first focus their message on the evils of solitary confinement and move on to other prison issues later.

Don't combine two events in one. For example, there's no reason to release a report about the benefits of recycling cans and announce the kickoff of a ballot initiative mandating recycling of cans at the same press conference. It's better to plan a press strategy involving the release of the report later in order to draw further attention to the ballot initiative.

After you have developed your message, build your media event around it. Everything about your event should help communicate this message—the site, the speakers, the sound bites, the signs, the images associated with the event itself—every possible detail.

2

Decide If a Media Event
Is Right for You

BEFORE YOU PLUNGE INTO organizing a media event, think about what you want to accomplish beyond simply getting in the news.

Who's Your Audience?

Make sure your media event will reach the right people. It's not always necessary to send a message through the media to the widest audience. Sometimes, depending on your strategy, you may need to reach citizens in a defined area such as the district of a specific state legislator. If so, publishing a guest opinion or letter to the editor in a small community newspaper in the legislator's district may be more effective than staging a telegenic media event. (See Chapter 37, "Landing on *Oprah* Is Not a Strategy.")

As you select media events, make sure your image and message are appropriate for your target audience, whether a certain demographic group or a particular policymaker. For example, if you're trying to send a message about birth control to teenagers, you'd probably want to focus on pop radio instead of the newspaper.

Ask yourself, Who's my target audience? What type of media do they read, watch, or listen to? What image is appropriate for them? If your strategy dictates that you reach only a segment of your community, use specific media outlets that will reach your target group.

Enough Money, People, Time?

The most common stumbling blocks to organizing a successful media event are money, people, and time. Different kinds of events require different amounts of each. Choose an event that matches your resources.

Bankrolling an expensive event yourself can be a disaster, leaving you burned out and disillusioned. Think carefully about all the expenses associated with your media event from beginning to end and have a realistic plan for raising the money. Costs can add up quickly. Consider, among other possible expenses, printing, insurance, supplies, phone calls, and transportation.

Make sure you can count on the people you think you can count on. If you select an event that requires 100 people, make sure you've got that much support.

Sometimes it's worth taking a risk and organizing a media event that may "fail" for whatever reasons (e.g., no people, lack of funds, no coverage, bad weather). But most of the time, it's best to limit the risk of failure because a media event that's a bust can set your cause back. And it's easy enough to generate coverage with events that are less likely to fail.

If, for example, you tell the press you can rally enough people to encircle a toxic plant and you fail, the headline in the next day's paper will look like this, as it did in the *Denver Post* in 1989, "Protesters Settle for Broken Circle; 4,200 Turnout for Rally Falls Short." The lead paragraph read: "An estimated 4,200 antinuclear demonstrators, trying to stretch the human chain with bedspreads, banners and even long-stemmed flowers, watched in disappointment yesterday as a planned encirclement of Rocky Flats fizzled into a broken line of protest."

This "negative" coverage can create the impression that your cause lacks support, which in this case was particularly irritating because a turnout of 4,200 people for a political event is excellent. Negative coverage can also cause volunteers to drop out or cause potential volunteers to seek groups that appear more successful.

However, if you are too worried about failing, you may miss a chance for big success. Big risks—expecting 20,000 to turn out for a rally—can have big payoffs. For example, the Million Man March in 1996 in Washington, D.C., had far fewer than a million people, but that didn't diminish its media coverage. Also consider that a creative, low-budget, "small time" event can generate more coverage than an expensive, complicated event that may fail. A rule of thumb: It's far better if 150 people show up at a meeting venue that seats 100 than if 150 people partially fill a cavernous hall designed for 500 people.

Will the event be fun? It's a great idea to decide against organizing an event that won't be any fun. Who wants to confirm the stereotype of an angry, bored, foaming-at-the-mouth, and unhappy community organizer? Remember that author and anarchist Emma Goldman said if she couldn't dance, she didn't want to be in the revolution.

3

Determine What's Newsworthy

DESPITE A LIBRARY OF BOOKS addressing the issue, there is no clear definition of "news." My favorite is Leon V. Sigal's in his book *Reporters and Officials*. The definition of news, he observes, is what's in the news.

Clearly, Sigal's definition is not all that helpful. But it seems the definition of news is just as murky for journalists, who decide what's news every day. For example, one young TV news reporter told an activist friend of mine that she was confused about how "news" was defined at her TV station in Los Angeles. Whenever she asked her boss if a particular story was newsworthy, he would ask her, "Does it wiggle?" What does this mean? Who knows.

I asked some of the journalists I interviewed for this book what "newsworthy" meant to them:

"What's newsworthy?" asks Keith Rogers, a reporter for the *Las Vegas Review Journal*. "You have to look at your audience. We're touching people's lives who read the newspaper."

"Every news day is different," says Cathy McFeaters, news director for KVUE-TV in Austin, the ABC affiliate. "And every situation is different. That's the thing about news. I always get nervous when I hear simple definitions of what news is."

"If it's Sunday and nothing is happening, anything can be news," says Krystian Orlinski, a Los Angeles–based editor for Reuters Television, a news service.

"The sexy and trendy and interesting stuff will take precedence over the long-range stuff," says *Denver Post* reporter Jack Cox. "That's how news decisions are made."

In the end, defining "newsworthy" is more of an intuitive process than a rational one. The more news you consume, the easier it will be for you to understand what's news to different news outlets.

Characteristics of a Newsworthy Event

There are a number of characteristics commonly associated with a "news" story. The more of these characteristics connected with an event, the more coverage it will likely get:

Novelty
Shock
Conflict
New data
Simplicity
Kids
Social issues or a prominent public figure involved
Humor
Outdoor location
Action
Bright props and images
News stories about the event published in advance
Local impact
A symbol of a trend
Holidays, anniversaries

Following are some characteristics of an event that will keep many journalists away:

Indoor location
People reading scripts
A private, profit-oriented goal
Complexity
Unknown participants
Bad timing or remote location

A story with credible, new data about a timely subject is often of most interest to a print reporter and not necessarily of interest to a television reporter, who needs visual imagery. If you've got new information and a visual to go along with it, you've got the strongest story for the widest variety of journalists.

However, even stories *without* "hard" data are widely covered by all kinds of media. Image-based or ironic stories can be just as newsworthy as a 250-page report full of new statistics.

Images for Television

From parenting to politics, television is clearly the most dominant force in American life. If you want to communicate with most Americans, you have to use images and symbols that can be beamed through the tube. (See Chapter 4, "Create Newsworthy Visual Imagery, Symbols, and Stunts.")

"The question is not what you want to say, but what you will be able to *show*," says Claus Kleber, a Washington, D.C., correspondent for KRD, German public television. "Come up with something visual."

"A meeting, I don't care about," says Deborah Clayton, an assignment editor for KVBC-TV, the NBC affiliate in Las Vegas. "Television needs to be visually stimulating."

"If it doesn't have good pictures, people won't put it on the air," says Peter Dykstra, a senior producer for Cable News Network in Atlanta.

Eat Bread, Water, and the News

Probably the best way to understand news is to absorb as much of it from as many media outlets as you can stomach. That means a wide variety—television, radio, dailies, weeklies, freebies. You have to know what "news" is being dished out to the public. Then you can match what you're publicizing with media that might bite. More important, you will be able to develop a sense for what's "news" for various media outlets and develop events and stories accordingly.

Practice thinking like a journalist. Here's an example of the journalistic mind at work: Rocky Mountain Peace and Justice Center staffer Tom Marshall was once trying to convince a CBS News producer to do a story on transport of nuclear waste from Denver to southern New Mexico. The producer listened to Tom and said she wanted to show the possible impacts on children. "Is there a school on the route?" she asked.

Connect a Stunt to a Newsworthy Event

Many journalists make a distinction between a "stunt" and "news." News, in this view, is new, "credible" information, possibly based on government documents or statistics. A stunt is a quirky, often humorous or image-based event—usually staged by a marginal group. An example of a stunt is a rally by five activists in penguin costumes trying to draw attention to the slaughter of these birds.

"I much prefer news to stunts, but I like a good stunt, too. But a quality stunt is hard to pull off. . . . If a stunt is significantly disruptive of daily life it can't be ignored," says John Fleck, a reporter with the *Albuquerque Journal*.

The distinction between news and a stunt is hard to pinpoint because "news" often derives its newsworthiness from its source, not its substance. For better or worse, statements by officials, even if they are blatantly misleading or incorrect, are closer to the "news" category in the eyes of many journalists regardless of the content of the information or the intentions of the official source.

"You get a call from the U.S. Treasury and you're going to listen much more closely than to a call from Greenpeace," says Michael Hirsh, a Washington, D.C., correspondent for *Newsweek*. As a result of this type of thinking, stunts *by activists* are sometimes viewed by journalists as less newsworthy than stunts by government officials (e.g., the mayor goes to the park to pick up trash).

Arrests can make stunts by activists more newsworthy—perhaps elevating them out of the stunt category altogether. "I wouldn't encourage people to get arrested," says Greg Todd, a former editor for the *Rocky Mountain News*, "but that definitely adds to the news value of the story."

For television, stunts can be much more effective. This is because television news often derives its newsworthiness from imagery, not necessarily from the importance of the information. Television journalists, with their thirst for images, may organize an entire story around one photogenic stunt.

Some argue that the news value of stunts has decreased in recent years. This may be true at the national level, but local media outlets—particularly local television news—still cover stunts widely. And interest in stunts by both national and local media can still be intense if you stage them at the right time.

For both television and print media, the news value of a stunt can be increased substantially if it's connected with a "more legitimate" event that will likely be in the news anyway. By connecting your event to a "news peg," you do not have to convince reporters that it's a good time to cover your issue—because it's already on their agendas. You simply have to convince them to cover your perspective. A stunt offers them the opportunity to do this—and a way to *illustrate* their stories.

"Everybody likes photos to illustrate stories, especially political stories which can be a bit dull," says Jon Craig, deputy political editor for the *Daily Express* in London. For example, opponents of the death penalty have a tough time attracting media attention. Their numbers are small and their cause unpopular. But a simple rally on the day that convicted Oklahoma City bomber Timothy McVeigh was sentenced to die attracted dozens of reporters around a small band of sign-carrying activists. One man, carrying a sign that read "WHAT WOULD JESUS DO?" was mobbed by reporters.

Similarly, Planned Parenthood activists knew that TV reporters would be looking for a "local reaction" to the state of the union address, in which the president was going to make a controversial statement about abortion. The activists offered the reporters an image, inviting them to one of their homes while they watched the speech. It worked. The activists were pictured on TV reacting positively to the president's statements about abortion rights.

Antismoking activists also took advantage of a news peg when news broke about poisons in food. *Media Advocacy and Public Health* describes how activists held a simple news conference after the federal government halted all imports of Chilean fruit because cyanide was discovered on some Chilean grapes. At the news conference, the activists displayed a cigarette and a bushel of Chilean grapes. They explained that one cigarette had more cyanide than one bushel of grapes. Yet the federal government was not acting to stop people from smoking cigarettes.

Following are some news pegs that make stunts newsworthy:

A public hearing
A court decision
The passage of a bill
A veto
A major speech
The release of a report
An anniversary of a historic event
A nomination

The best news pegs are *not* the ones that will be targeted by every other interest group. Many activists and organizations try to connect their issue to giant news pegs, like the arrival of the president to their town. A circus of stunters creates such intense competition that many are shut out of the news.

4

Create Newsworthy
Visual Imagery, Symbols,
and Stunts

THE MOST IMAGINATIVE and theatrical people are going to win," says Colin Covert, a feature reporter at the *Star Tribune* in Minneapolis. "Don't expect good intentions to get you space. The fact that you're trying to fight cancer is great, but it's not news. If you do something interesting, we'll write about it."

Successful media events are, above all else, *entertaining*. That doesn't necessarily mean *amusing*. In fact, some successful media events are somewhat disgusting. But whether amusing or disgusting—they are *engaging*, and that is the key synonym for entertainment in the news business.

In this chapter, which could be titled "Media Stunts for Anybody with a Cause," I will help you create symbols and imagery that will carry your cause into the news. A lot of my advice is oriented to television, but much of it can be used for print media as well.

Stop Being a Bore

When I lecture and hold workshops, I emphasize the importance of creating engaging events. Most everyone nods in agreement and then continues to generate the same boring news releases and events.

Many nonprofit professionals see my slide show—depicting activists dressing as pigs, delivering coffins, dropping banners from buildings—and say to me, "That's great for some small, alienated organization, but we want to communicate to middle America. And we want to remain *credible*."

This unfortunate thinking helps keep cause-oriented groups on the sidelines of society. Communicating with stunts is mainstream fare and has been for years. Politics has been reduced largely to a clash of symbols and symbolic actions.

Mainstream politicians use costumes to create imagery. There are many examples, but here are three: (1) One of the lasting images of President Clinton's 1996 campaign against Sen. Bob Dole was the Democratic National Committee's use of "Buttman," a party activist dressed in a cigarette-butt costume. Buttman dogged Dole around the country, linking him to the tobacco companies. (2) Not long before Buttman emerged, Rep. Patricia Schroeder appeared at a news conference with the "sacred cow" to communicate her message that certain items in the federal budget were not on the cutting block. (3)The reelection campaign of Gov. Roy Romer of Colorado sent a "duck" to the rallies of his opponent to drive home Romer's point that his opponent was "ducking" his challenge to debate.

In any case, the point is that "serious" and "credible" communication is not limited to words. Images and symbols communicate to everyone. They are the lowest common denominator in communications.

Examples of Successful Media Events

In this section are media events that have generated news coverage and some examples of how citizens have altered proven tactics to fit their issue. In most cases, the same idea has been used by

To focus the media spotlight on Sen. Bob Dole's ties to tobacco companies, a Democratic Party activist dressed as Buttman. Credit: Mike Altschule

activists representing completely different causes.

To create an event, consider assembling a group for a brainstorming session. I'm generally not a big fan of doing tasks in large groups, but this really works: Read each of the following descriptions of media events and then write down everyone's ideas for adapting it to your cause. Write down every idea conceived during the brainstorm without criticizing it, without getting more details, and without exploring the pros and cons. As you think of ideas, do not get bogged down in logistics such as where the event would be held and who would bring props. After all the ideas are in, go back and decide what's doable and what will be newsworthy. The best stunts combine humor and conflict.

Cameras Love Costumes

In this age of theatrical "news" shows, it's easy to understand why costumes are a great tool to attract news cameras. They can be humorous, bright, lively, confrontational—all characteristics of a newsworthy event. And a very simple costume can be very effective; a one-dollar mask can get you on the evening news.

Rather than simply carrying a sign decrying pork-barrel spending on nuclear-bomb production, these activists attracted the news media with pig costumes. Credit: Jason Salzman

"Pigs" Oppose Pork-Barrel Politics. Federal spending for projects that are not truly needed but maintained to provide jobs is called "pork barrel" spending. At Greenpeace in Colorado, we had no tolerance for politicians who refused to call for the shutdown of unsafe nuclear-bomb making at the nearby Rocky Flats plant simply because the plant provided jobs. How did we make the point? Three activists dressed in larger-than-life fuzzy pink pig costumes that were rented from a costume shop. A dozen others donned simple pig noses. They snorted around in front of television cameras outside a dark auditorium where a not-made-for-TV hearing about Rocky Flats was taking place.

Is There a Santa Claus?   In Indianapolis, Indiana, citizens were upset over the high utility rates set by the Public Utilities Commission. They wanted the public to understand that the commission was allowing power companies to make huge profits at its expense. So during a July public hearing, Santa Claus showed up. "He walked into the hearing room and sat down right next to the commissioners," says organizer David Culp. "It brought the whole thing to a screeching halt. People did not know what to do." The message as reported by the media: The commissioners were being Santa Claus to private power companies by allowing them to charge high rates.

Clowns, Lemons, Gags, and Animals.   Activists have dressed as clowns (stop clowning around in the legislature), hazardous-waste workers (beware of a toxic danger), trees (stop clear-cutting), lemons (the nuclear reactor is a lemon; "nukes are sour, wind is power"), and almost anything else you can think of. A gag across the mouth creates a visual image of citizens being excluded from a debate for whatever reason. Animals strike a responsive chord among people.

Dramatize a Popular Expression

When you dramatize popular expressions with props and costumes, you can create ironic humor and conflict that make news. The key is to think of an expression, cliché, or idiom that both describes the essential message of your event *and* lends itself to being acted out or somehow made literal. Sometimes the phrase you're looking for is right in front of you because you use it every time you talk about your issue (e.g., "I know the governor's in bed with them!"). Other times you'll have to brainstorm long and hard to come up with the proper expression to dramatize. Once you've got the right expression, costumes are usually called for. But they do not have to be elaborate. Sometimes just big name tags around the necks of activists-actors will do the trick.

In Bed with Polluters.   It was clear to activists in Arizona that officials from the state's environmental agencies were ignoring their concerns because of their cozy relationship with a large company proposing to build an incinerator in the state. To make this point to the public, they put the government agencies in bed with the polluters, literally. They hauled a bed to the steps of the state capitol, put effigies of the polluters and the officials in it, and announced they would remain there "until the government gets out of bed with polluters." Fake money streamed out of the pockets of the "polluters," and the protesters used giant blowups of dollar bills as backdrops. Other signs read "Why are government agencies in bed with the polluters?" During the seven-day protest, the activists generated major local coverage, including live telecasts and daily updates from "The Bed." Sound bites: "The government isn't even taking precautions" and "Politics makes for strange bedfellows, but the adage has never been demonstrated more explicitly."

Waffling on the Issues.   In a display of creativity on the campaign trail, one candidate in a 1992 congressional race held a press conference in front of a waffle house to dramatize the point that his opponent was "waffling on the issues."

Red Tape, Alka-Seltzer, Chickens, Shredder, and Bullshit.   AIDS activists, critical of the federal government's long process for analyzing drugs before they were released to the public, wrapped themselves in red tape to illustrate that government "red tape" was costing lives. Planned Parenthood activists dropped Alka-Seltzer into a glass of water to show that antiabortion protests had "fizzled." Activists have dressed as chickens to illustrate the point that a politician is too "chicken" to take on a tough issue. They rented a tree shredder, the kind used by tree-trimming companies to shred branches, to illustrate that international trade agreements would "shred" environmental laws. Finally, environmental activists thought Sen. Dianne Feinstein's compromise on a logging issue was "bullshit." Guess what they dumped in front of her office.

The Worst or the Best: You Give the Grades

The media love winners and losers. The bigger, the better. What better way to illustrate that someone's a total failure than to give him or her an "F" or an award for being despicable? Conversely, an opportunity for a photo of a politician receiving flowers for outstanding behavior may be hard for the news media to pass up. And it's the type of image the public tends to remember.

The Dirty Dozen.   Each year for over twenty years, Environmental Action in Washington, D.C., has inducted twelve members of Congress into an elite club: the Dirty Dozen. These lawmakers are, in Environmental Action's opinion, the most offensive enemies of the environment to (dis)grace the halls of Congress. Environmental Action consistently generates national news coverage from this event.

Report Card for the Energy Secretary.   In an effort to draw attention to the poor performance of Energy Secretary James Watkins, the Military Production Network, a national alliance of citizens' organizations, presented him with a "report card." The network invited the news media to witness the presentation of the report card, which appeared in the *Washington Post* with this sound bite from Idaho organizer Liz Paul: "If I came home with that report card, I'd have been grounded for the summer, had my allowance cut, and had the car keys taken away."

A Ticket, Flowers, and More.   Activists have presented flowers to the French ambassador after France announced a moratorium on nuclear testing; "gas-guzzling violations" to low-mileage cars; an annual "burned-out lightbulb" award to a legislator; and Valentine's Day gifts to favorite public servants.

Signs in the Windows

Any segment of the community—businesses, civic groups, doctors, senior citizens, chambers of commerce, or religious or youth groups—can be organized around a resolution or common statement of concern. But rather than having community members sign a piece of paper, think of ways to make their sentiments visual.

"As a businessperson, I thought we had something at stake," explains activist Richard Johnson, who founded Another Business Against WIPP (Waste Isolation Pilot Plant) as part of his efforts to stop a radioactive waste dump in New Mexico. "It was a matter of awakening the same feeling in other businesspeople." Johnson succeeded. About 600 businesses are listed in the directory of Another Business Against WIPP. Each of these businesses allows its name to be given to the media and listed in newspaper ads. Most businesses place a small sign (Another Business Against WIPP) in their windows. Also, they agree to give 5 percent of gross sales two days per year to Concerned Citizens for Nuclear Safety, a Santa Fe group opposing WIPP. In turn, Concerned Citizens encourages its members and the public to patronize bussinesses associated with Another Business Against WIPP throughout the year, particularly on the designated 5 percent days. "It's become good business to be a business against WIPP," says Johnson. He adds that the involvement by businesses brought WIPP opposition into the mainstream and "made it safe" for the city council, school board, and chamber of commerce to endorse anti-WIPP resolutions.

Make the Most of a Petition

Some activists collect signatures to put an issue on the election ballot. These petitions are meticulously counted and regulated according to election rules. Undertaking a ballot initiative is a major campaign, and the formal presentation of the required signatures, usually to the secretary of state's office, is often noted by the media.

Most activists, however, circulate petitions simply to draw attention to a problem. Unfortunately, after arriving in a politician's mailbox, these petitions often go straight into the trash can or, if we're lucky, the recycling bin.

Petitions should be delivered in a way that creates an image and drama for the news media. Deliver petitions inside something (e.g., a coffin, trash can, or symbol of your issue). Or simply make the petitions visible somehow.

Another way to make petitions more newsworthy is to have your petition focus on some other body besides the government (e.g., a hospital, senior center, school, or chamber of commerce). You can also write creative petition questions that may be more newsworthy.

A Petition Carpet.   Greenpeace activists collected over 100,000 signatures to pressure the government to stop nuclear weapons production. It was my job to decide how to attract media attention to the presentation of the petitions. I decided to create a carpet by taping the letter-sized petitions onto cheap burlap fabric. We stretched the carpet from the governor of Colorado's car to the doors of the state capitol. An insider gave us a tip that the governor would be going to his car at a certain hour, and we hoped he would step on our "carpet," illustrating our point that he was "trampling on the will of the people" by not calling for the shutdown of nuclear-bomb production. Instead, the governor's press secretary greeted us and a handful of photographers. I thought she would have enough media savvy not to step on the petition carpet, but she plunked her foot right down on it. Her photo was on the front page of one local newspaper.

A Petition Roll.   The AFL-CIO obtained hundreds of signatures on a thirty-six-inch-wide roll of paper, which was unfurled on the Capitol steps in Washington, D.C. An Associated Press photo of it appeared in papers across the United States.

A Petition Drape and Petition Bags.   Instead of quietly delivering petitions to politicians, pro-choice activists in Kansas City received substantial media coverage by simply draping taped petitions over the railings of the capitol rotunda. Environmental activists, led by the Public Interest Research Group, stuffed thousands of petitions in bags and assembled them on the steps of the Capitol, generating a national AP photo.

Drop a Banner

Banners have been dropped from every kind of structure in support of every conceivable cause. You'd think their news value would have vanished, but in most cases it hasn't. A banner unveiled at the right moment in the right place can generate a lot of attention in most media markets, even though this tactic has been used repeatedly. When all else fails, you don't even need a banner. Hold up a large sign. Never underestimate the power of signs as news, especially if the timing is right.

"Next Time . . . Try Recycling."   In September 1986, a garbage barge crept out of New York Harbor and embarked on an eleven-month worldwide search for a dumpsite for its cargo of household waste. As each government rejected the barge, the international media frenzy around it grew. By the time the barge returned to New York in August 1987, it had become the object of a full-court international media event. It had become a symbol of the "garbage problem." As it floated in New York Harbor, waiting for instructions on what to do next, two Greenpeace activists swam out to it with a banner. The media were notified, and with photographers assembled, the activists unveiled the banner against the backdrop of garbage: "Next Time . . . Try Recycling." The photo of this event became an instant worldwide media hit.

More Banner Ideas.   Activists have climbed existing billboards and covered them with their own banners (covering any existing

Greenpeace targeted a garbage barge to focus the attention of the news media on the need for recycling. Credit: Greenpeace/Dennis Capalongo

sign with *your* sign can make news); dropped banners from construction sites; put letters on people's shirts (one letter per shirt) and made a human banner; and placed photos of women who have had breast cancer on a banner.

Stage a Roadside Protest and Call Traffic Reporters

Radio audiences are at their peak during "drive time," which occurs about 7 A.M. to 9 A.M. and 4 P.M. to 6 P.M. or later, and a fixture on most popular radio stations during these hours is traffic reports. If you can somehow inject your message into the traffic reports, you will reach a huge radio audience. It turns out that this is not as difficult as you might think. Traffic reports, you will notice, frequently broadcast traffic problems phoned in by drivers. If you create a traffic-related "problem," which actually may not disrupt traffic at all, you can worm your way into the traffic reports. How to do it? Stage a protest by the side of the highway and call the traffic reporters. This works. As one veteran radio reporter told me, "If you're climbing a billboard along the highway, people will call us on their cell phones."

One Friday morning in 1993, ten freeway overpasses in southern California carried more than commuter traffic: Banners were slung on the overpasses, facing the freeway below, protesting Governor Pete Wilson's proposal to construct a waste dump in southern California. The banners read "Wilson: Stop Your Nuclear Dump." The protest received widespread attention because the traffic reports on the morning radio shows announced the presence of the banners repeatedly, in part because activists and drivers with cellular phones made sure the radio stations knew about them. Activists estimate that they reached millions of people in southern California that morning.

Create a Replica of the Problem

Many political problems remain unsolved because the public literally can't see them. If problems become visible—and accessible to photographers and the media—the political will to solve them is much more likely to materialize.

Recognizing this, activists find ways to move social ills from behind locked doors into the public domain—into our communal backyard. One way to do this is to create a replica of the problem. The following media events involve three types of replicas: In the first three, activists employed realistic replicas; in the fourth, a larger-than-life replica was used; and in the last two they used replicas of disasters to make their point.

Amber Waves of Grain.   After viewing artist Barbara Donachy's 34,000 miniature clay bombs and submarines representing the entire U.S. nuclear arsenal, a teacher told Donachy: "Wow, I thought we only had 100 bombs. It's good to have something like this so

A 34,000-piece replica of the U.S. nuclear arsenal, composed of miniature clay bombs and submarines, generated international news coverage. Credit: Barbara Donachy

people know." Designed to present a realistic visual image of U.S. nuclear weaponry, it was shown across this country and abroad during the height of the Cold War. The mottled patterns of the cones and their shadows covering 5,000 square feet inspired the name *Amber Waves of Grain*. The piece is now permanently displayed at the National Peace Museum in Nebraska.

Mock Nuclear Waste Cask.   For years, activists in Nevada struggled to expand public opposition to the proposed Yucca Mountain nuclear waste dump near Las Vegas. The dump would hold radioactive waste from nuclear reactors across the United States. They decided to draw wider attention to the problem by highlighting the highways on which the waste would be transported to Nevada. To do this, they built a full-sized, mock transport cask. They trucked it to rallies and toured around the United States with it, generating news coverage at most stops.

Shanty Towns and Animals.   In the mid-1980s students opposing apartheid in South Africa constructed "shanty towns" in public places to depict living conditions for blacks in South Africa. Animal-rights groups have created papier-mâché animals to draw attention to their demonstrations.

A Giant Radioactive Waste Barrel.   I try to figure out how low-budget variations of advertising tricks can work for nonprofit organizations. Once I was skiing at a Colorado resort and was appalled to see a giant beer can and a giant gorilla with a radio station's name on it nestled in the trees below the chairlift. The twenty-foot inflatable beer can was just like the ones you see at street fairs, but it looked uglier in the forest—even if it was on the side of a ski slope. In any case, I saw the giant can and said to myself, "Maybe Greenpeace can get one of those." I checked around and found out that custom-made, they were $5,000 or more. I eventually found a Greenpeace volunteer who had worked for one of the companies that manufacture these inflatables. She made us a twenty-foot-tall "inflatable radioactive waste barrel." It was radioactive yellow with a black-and-white radiation symbol painted on it. Every time we faced a fight over radioactive waste, we hauled out the giant barrel, "dumping" it on the capitol steps in different cities. And nearly every time, it was a media hit, generating huge amounts of free publicity.

A Polluting Incinerator.   According to activists, Bill Clinton and Al Gore promised during their first election campaign to shut down a controversial hazardous-waste incinerator in Ohio. Activists there were outraged when the administration failed to keep its promise. Joining other groups, they handcuffed themselves to a mock incinerator parked on the street in front of the White House. The incinerator belched "noxious" smoke and was emblazoned with the words "Clinton-Gore Keep Your Word, SHUT IT DOWN."

Exploding Nuclear Reactor, a Car Wreck, and Airborn Toxic Emissions. Activists in South Carolina created a ten-foot-high nuclear reactor equipped with a siren and fire extinguisher for mock explosions to demonstrate the danger posed by nuclear reactors at the Savannah River nuclear-bomb plant. Other activists have staged a mock car crash on a busy street to highlight the danger of cars and released helium balloons to show how winds carry toxic emissions.

Depict a Symbol of Your Concerns

A variation on replicating the problem is to create a visual representation of a symbol of your concerns. To do this, make a list of everything associated with your concerns and figure out if anything could be depicted visually *and* would successfully illustrate the message you want conveyed through the news media. Frequently, the media make thinking of symbols easy because they may have already identified them and focused on them, but they may not have access to imagery of the symbols that they've already made people aware of.

Imelda's Shoes. Imelda Marcos, wife of former Filipino dictator Ferdinand Marcos, had a collection of 1,200 pairs of shoes, discovered when Marcos fled the Philippines. The shoe stockpile, once it was revealed, became a symbol of the excesses of the Marcos regime. Filipino activists built a "monument of shame" composed of shoes and shoe boxes to draw attention to the suffering of the Filipino people as a result of the Marcos dictatorship. They constructed the monument after it was revealed that the former first lady of the Philippines spent over $5,000 on crocodile-leather shoes during a visit to Hong Kong to retrieve money stashed in bank accounts there.

Gun Victims' Shoes. Shootings and killings are ubiquitous in the news, particularly on local television news. But how often do you see protests about guns? And if you do, how often do they make an impact that lasts? The Coalition to Stop Gun Violence searched for a symbol that could pierce the numbness many of us have developed about violent crime. It assembled 40,000 pairs of shoes of citizens killed by guns. The protest was covered by many news outlets.

Empty Chairs, Chain Saws, and Silhouettes. University students assembled 100 empty chairs on the campus lawn, symbolizing the estimated 100 students who were denied admission due to lack of financial aid; leaders of environmental groups rallied, with chain saws in their hands, to call for restrictions on clearcutting; and domestic-violence opponents marked Domestic-Violence Prevention Month by placing cardboard silhouettes of fifty domestic-violence victims on the Colorado capitol lawn.

Expose the Actual Problem

Rather than expose a symbol of the problem you face, you can expose or reveal the actual problem in a public place. Of course, this is not an option if your problem doesn't exist yet or if it is impossible to make it available for journalists to see. But here are some examples of how activists successfully exposed real problems.

Crawling for Access. As part of their campaign to obtain access to the Colorado capitol, activists for organizations representing people with disabilities decided they would expose the problem.

Because there was insufficient wheelchair access, they abandoned their wheelchairs and tried to crawl up the steps of the capitol with a throng of TV cameras in tow. On the backs of their shirts, they wrote, "Why must we crawl?" At the time they staged their protest, the legislature was considering a bill to provide funds to modify the capitol for access.

Lemonade with a Twist.   "Would you or any members of your court like a drink?" asked Radford Lyons, age eight, at a public hearing. He then offered the hearing officials free lemonade made from contaminated well water in Pike County, Kentucky. The protest was part of a campaign by Kentuckians for the commonwealth to have water lines extended to homes in the area of the contaminated wells. At the end of the hearing, one official promised to have the water lines constructed.[1]

Real and Toy Guns.   *Media Advocacy and Public Health* describes how an emergency room doctor in California focused media attention on the need for laws restricting access to guns. His research showed that every year in California, dozens of children accidentally shot other children or themselves. One of the reasons was that real guns look like toy guns. To illustrate this, the doctor mounted real guns and toy guns on plywood and at a news conference asked reporters to distinguish between the two. This generated wide coverage.

Vote on It

A vote is a great way to transform an idea into an event that can be covered by the media. Not only does a vote clearly identify winners and losers for journalists, it also adds credibility to "fringe" positions. Voting is a respectable, thoroughly accepted way to decide any question. A vote of an entire town or state is of obvious news value, but even a ballot question put before a church or temple, school, civic group, or senior center can be newsworthy. For example, a petition with 100 signatures has less news value than a vote of 100 members of a church.

"Suicide Pills" for Use After Nuclear War.   When I was a student at Brown University in 1982, the threat of nuclear war was at its peak. Members of the Reagan administration openly talked about fighting and winning a nuclear battle. Meanwhile, the antinuclear movement, which gained national momentum around the idea of freezing the arms race, had begun to decline. I didn't understand how this could be so. The only explanation I could come up with was that the possibility of nuclear war was too abstract for people to understand. This meant that as antinuclear activists, our challenge was to bring the problem home somehow. Looking around the campus, I observed that signs identified dormitory basements as fallout shelters for use by students during nuclear war. I phoned the Federal Emergency Management Agency in downtown Providence, and it confirmed that the fallout shelters in the dorms were still part of the nation's defense against nuclear attack. As part of my activities with the Brown Disarmament Group, I led a petition drive calling on university president Howard Swearer to declare the fallout shelters useless for nuclear-war survival. Think about it: Could students survive a nuclear war in a dorm basement? Despite 1,000 student signatures, Swearer refused to make this declaration, telling me that he would consider the move if other Ivy League schools joined Brown. This was totally absurd, but what could I do? Most of my fellow disarmament activists thought that focusing on fallout shelters was a waste of time anyway. So I gave up and pursued another course: During the fallout shelter campaign, one student told me she'd prefer to have a suicide pill than hide in a fallout shelter. Though it sounds sort of crazy, this made sense to me. So I and some friends formed a new group, Students for Suicide Tablets. Our

group collected 700 signatures to put the following item on the student council election ballot: "We, the undergraduate students of Brown University, request that Brown University Health Services stockpile suicide pills for optional student use exclusively in the event of a nuclear war." Once the measure was on the ballot, it was picked up by the *Providence Journal*, which learned about it from the *Brown Daily Herald*. The following day, the Associated Press called about the story, and by noon CBS News was on campus. Soon, we had spoken to journalists from most major media outlets in the United States. We were even guests on the Donahue show. In the following weeks on campus, students debated how they should vote on the suicide-pill measure. Most of the 700 students who had originally signed the suicide-pill petition, allowing the question to appear on the ballot, did so not because they wanted the pills but because they agreed that there was no harm in letting students vote on it. Initially, there was little support for the pills on campus. In fact, many heard about the issue only when fearful parents called to ask about the problem at school. The director of Student Health Services, Dr. Sumner Hoffman, unwittingly stoked the already intense media frenzy around the upcoming vote by declaring his opposition to it: "Our mission is to sustain life, to improve the quality of life, to treat illness, not to destroy life." The university's spokesperson simply said, "No pills." He also tried to explain that he believed the students were motivated by "serious concerns" about nuclear war. Most students agreed and accepted the suicide pills as a symbol even though our group said the pills were both a symbol and a real request. In the end, in April 1982, students voted 60–40 percent for the pills. The results were announced by Dan Rather that evening. Brown never stocked the pills.

Referendums on "Sanctuaries" and "Freezing the Arms Race."
Activists concerned about U.S. policy in Central America staged referendums in the 1980s to draw attention to their cause. They

voted on whether their places of worship, colleges, and other institutions should be "sanctuaries" for refugees from Central American countries. This "sanctuary movement" received a lot of press coverage. Similarly, activists in the 1980s first drew attention to the idea of freezing the production of nuclear warheads by staging referendums at town meetings in small New England towns. Eventually, entire states voted to "freeze the arms race," but the U.S. House of Representatives voted down the measure.

A Celebrity Endorsement

Take advantage of our society's obsession with sports and Hollywood. Finding a celebrity or notable person to endorse your cause or speak at your event can be difficult, but it's worth the effort. I've seen a celebrity join a cause and suddenly change everything. Support comes out of nowhere. Your position becomes credible.

"Celebrities help stories," says Jon Craig, deputy political editor of the *Daily Express* in London. "I'm sure interest groups know that. If you've got Arnold Schwarzenegger or somebody famous to back your campaign, it helps."

Bonnie Raitt and Soul Asylum.   After struggling to raise the profile of the fight against a nuclear-waste dump proposed by Northern States Power near the Mississippi River, activists in Minnesota enlisted Bonnie Raitt and Soul Asylum to perform at the state capitol on "Stop the Dump! Citizens' Lobbying Day." They played a benefit concert, which they called "Night to Send a Message," and it generated intense print and broadcast coverage. The presence of the celebrity rock stars completely changed the debate about the waste dump in Minnesota, transforming it into a mainstream cause. "I've run into all these situations where music has saved people, and music has changed the way people think," Dave Pirner of Soul Asylum told the *St. Paul Pioneer Press*.[2]

Mothers and Others.   Actress Meryl Streep joined a Mothers and Others for Pesticide Limits campaign against Alar, a pesticide used on apples. The campaign received major media attention.

Make Your Advertisement News

It's usually not a good idea for a small nonprofit organization to buy paid advertisements. Ads cost too much, especially if they are repeated enough times to make a dent in the minds of the targeted audience. A half-page ad in the *New York Times*, for example, costs tens of thousands of dollars. But paid ads do make sense if they create a controversy and therefore become news themselves, exponentially stretching your advertising dollar.

"Bob, I've Got Emphysema."   In the seventh year of its statewide antismoking campaign, the California Health Department decided to step up its advertising campaign. It sponsored a series of ads that left a trail of media coverage and debate in their wake. One billboard depicted what appeared to be "Marlboro Country." But instead, one of the Marlboro men was saying to the other, "Bob, I've got emphysema." Another hard-hitting TV ad showed a women whose larynx, or voice box, was removed because of the effects of throat cancer. But she continues to smoke through a hole in her throat, and she does so in the television ad.

Bleeding Buffalo.   In March 1997, the state of Montana killed hundreds of buffalo that had migrated out of Yellowstone National Park. Artist Steve Kelly was outraged by the killing and created two billboards depicting bleeding buffalo and the phrase "Grown in Yellowstone . . . Slaughtered in Montana." The billboards immediately became statewide news. A few months later, his billboards became news again after a chamber of commerce official left this message on Kelly's answering machine: "You need to call us right away, up here in Helena. . . . We will not tolerate that kind of ad-

Gamble Colorado

Colorado is waiting for you. In the winter, you'll find world-class skiing at numerous Rocky Mountain ski areas and snow-covered cross-country tracks. In the summer, the hiker and bicycle rider have plenty to do. Secluded trails and mountain peaks make a perfect get-away. The Colorado towns of Black Hawk and Central City allow tourists to try their luck at games of chance. And there is more. Coloradans are famous for their hospitality and concern for visitors. From gourmet Denver restaurants to remote bed-and-breakfast hotels, Colorado wants to make this year's vacation your best ever! Make your reservations today.

GREENPEACE
1021 PEARL STREET, SUITE 200
BOULDER, COLORADO 80302

WARNING: In 1992, the government plans to restart nuclear bomb production at the Rocky Flats Plant, located 20 miles from the Denver airport. But the plutonium plant violates certain environmental laws and does not meet all current safety standards, and there is no safe way to dispose of the dangerous radioactive waste piled up at Rocky Flats. If you care about Colorado – and especially if you plan to visit the Denver area – make sure Rocky Flats stays closed. Tell Colorado Gov. Roy Romer (303-866-2575) to oppose the restart of Rocky Flats.

A warning label similar to those found on cigarette packages made this mock tourist advertisement newsworthy. Credit: Greenpeace

vertisement in Helena. . . . It's in bad taste for tourists coming through town. We get complaints on it, and I'm going to forward all the telephone calls to you and let you justify it."[3]

Gamble Colorado. At Greenpeace, we placed an ad in the western edition of the *New York Times*, which is less expensive than other editions but still carries the credibility and "national" appeal of the *Times*. The ad, headlined "Gamble Colorado," lauded the virtues of a vacation in Colorado: "Colorado is waiting for you. In the winter, you'll find world-class skiing at numerous Rocky Mountain ski areas and snow-covered cross-country tracks. In the summer, the hiker and bicycle rider have plenty to do. Secluded trails and mountain peaks make a perfect get-away. The Colorado towns of Black Hawk and Central City allow tourists to try their luck at games of chance." However, it included a warning label—like the ones on cigarette cartons—advising tourists that Colorado might be unsafe to visit because of the Rocky Flats nuclear-bomb plant:

> "WARNING: In 1992, the government plans to restart nuclear bomb production at the Rocky Flats Plant, located 20 miles from the Denver airport. But the plutonium plant violates certain environmental laws

and does not meet all current safety standards, and there is no safe way to dispose of dangerous radioactive waste piled up at Rocky Flats. If you care about Colorado—and especially if you plan to visit the Denver area—make sure Rocky Flats stays closed. Tell Colorado Gov. Roy Romer (303-866-2575) to oppose the restart of Rocky Flats."

The ad was reprinted (for free) on the news pages of local papers and national advertising magazines. It also appeared on TV.

Furs, Skeletons, and a CEO.   Other newsworthy ads have featured bloody fur coats; bloody tennis shoes with the statement "Adidas uses the skin of slaughtered kangaroos"; "skeletons"; and a photo of the chief executive officer of Du Pont, who is blamed for contributing to ozone destruction.

Threaten to Advertise

Sometimes just threatening to advertise can be just as effective and much cheaper than actually placing advertisements. This is what you do: Produce a very slick ad that makes it appear that your group is aggressive, smart, savvy, and, above all, well financed. This is best accomplished by having a professional advertising agency produce your ad. Then identify the key executives or decisionmakers whose minds you need to change. Send them the ad in the mail with a note explaining your plans to place the ad soon. (Another option, pioneered by media activist Tony Schwartz, is to determine which radio station a specific politician or executive listens to and when he or she listens to it. Place your ad on that radio station at the appropriate time, creating the illusion that you have a much broader ad campaign than you've actually got.)

"You Should Listen to This Tape."   Food and Water, Inc., a small environmental group in Vermont, has campaigned intensively against food irradiation. As part of its campaign, Food and Water produced slick thirty-second radio spots explaining the evils of

food irradiation and how a boycott of supermarkets stocking ir-
radiated food would succeed. Copies of the ads were made on
cassette tapes and sent to thousands of executives in the food industry with a note saying: "You should listen to this tape. We
plan to run it on radio stations in your area soon."[4]

"An Honor Waiting to Be Yours."   As part of its campaign to
lower the consumption of fat by U.S. citizens, the Center for Science in the Public Interest developed a radio spot specifically targeting Fred Turner, chairman of the board of McDonald's. The ad,
as described in *Media Advocacy and Public Health*, explained that
the oil McDonald's used for frying was bad for Americans'
health. It concluded: "So, Mr. Turner, by simply using vegetable
oil instead of beef tallow, you would play a great role in making
people a lot healthier. That's an honor waiting to be yours."

Get Your Ad Rejected

Another way to make news with your advertisement and avoid
the high costs of actually placing ads is to develop an ad that you
know will be rejected by media outlets. Then hold a press conference lambasting the decision to reject your ad. This not only will
create news but may win support for your efforts from free-
speech supporters.

The Nose on My Face.   Typically, public service announcements
are mundane and noncontroversial. Greenpeace chose to offer TV
stations in Nevada and New Mexico a slick, controversial announcement that it knew would be rejected by most stations. The
Greenpeace public service announcement depicts a tense, packed
public meeting where a government spokesperson is speaking
about plans for a radioactive-waste dump. He asks citizens attending the meeting to trust him. But as he speaks, his nose begins to grow longer and longer like Pinocchio's and to glow a ra-

dioactive shade of green. Sure enough, most TV stations rejected the "public service announcement," but local newspapers ran articles about the rejected ad ("Air Time Sought for Anti-Nuclear Spot") and local TV stations' news shows ran the entire ad as part of the news coverage of the controversy.

Rejection and Reprisal. *Media Advocacy and Public Health* explains how Neighbor to Neighbor, a small nonprofit, developed a television ad calling on citizens to boycott Proctor and Gamble's Folgers coffee. Some stations rejected the ad, but one ran it. Procter & Gamble withdrew all advertising from this station. The combination of the rejection of the ad and Proctor and Gamble's response ignited national news coverage that the small group could never have afforded.[5]

Send Your Message Uniquely

Letter-writing campaigns can be effective, but they don't often grab much media attention. But many nonprofit groups have realized that augmenting a letter-writing campaign by delivering *something else* to a politician can make big news, especially if you deliver it when your issue is already in the news. Any object can be delivered.

A Coffin for the Senator. During a debate in Congress about whether gays should be allowed in the military, gay-rights groups tried to deliver a coffin to Sen. Sam Nunn of Georgia. The coffin, on which was inscribed "Beaten to Death by the U.S. Navy," was prominently featured in the *New York Times* amid a flood of stories about Nunn's opposition to President Bill Clinton's proposal to repeal the ban on gays serving in the armed forces. (A coffin can be purchased at a mortuary or constructed from cardboard.)

A Survival Kit. The Snake River Alliance campaigns to stop shipments of radioactive waste from entering Idaho. In late 1989, Idaho governor Cecil Andrus was under pressure from the Department of Energy to accept radioactive-waste shipments from other states. The Snake River Alliance sent the governor a letter accompanied by a "Fend Off the Feds Survival Kit." The kit contained, among other items, an arm sling, a red pen, and an oversized set of lips. The letter read, "Wear the enlarged lips to make it easy for federal officials to 'read your lips' when you say 'no' to nuclear waste. Use the red pen to write 'reject' on ill-conceived federal proposals to store waste in Idaho. And, in case your arm is sore after repeated twistings by federal officials, put it in the kit's sling and you'll recover quickly."

Hangers, Paper Plates, and Shells. Other activists have hand-delivered hangers, illustrating the ramifications of an abortion ban; paper plates, showing the plight of the hungry; and the ashes of cremated AIDS victims, highlighting policies related to the treatment of the disease.

Contact Elected Officials from the Street

Just as creativity helps make a rally newsworthy, it can turn a letter-writing campaign into news. One way is to simply write letters—or notify politicians of your concerns—in a public place.

A Fax Machine on the Street. Journalists wrote about three activists with signs and a portable fax machine in the street, urging citizens to fax letters to Congress. What's the news value? It was probably a slow news day, which can mean that an easy story like this can make news. "I might be sitting there and it's a dead day," says Craig Maclaine, a reporter for Radio Canada International, an arm of the Canadian Broadcasting Corporation. "What am I going to cover?"

Public E-mailing or Cell Phone Calling. Citizens have made news with rather tame gatherings in public places to call their elected officials on cell phones.

March the Distance

A more newsworthy variation of a rally is a march. Even a fifteen-minute march has a bit more visual appeal than a rally, but a long march of a day or more is more interesting to journalists. It generates more unexpected stories and visual images, particularly if you add a creative twist such as "marching" on Roller Blades. And it illustrates a bit more commitment. If you've got only a few dozen people and they're committed, you're probably better off with a long march than a rally.

Students March for Three Days.   A teacher in a large metropolitan school district led a group of fifty students on a three-day, sixty-mile march to protest cuts in the education budget. As they approached the capitol, carrying signs such as "Your Future Depends on My Education," the high school students were joined by 150 more of their peers. Along the way, their saga—sore ankles, sunburn, and other discomforts—attracted the full flock of local media. A series of stories appeared, starting when they began their march and concluding with their rally at the capitol, which was attended by a few state legislators.

Cross-Country Activist.   You periodically see stories in the local media about the lone activist or small group that's on a cross-country trek for justice. For example, one activist recently made himself known to local media as he biked and hiked from Seattle to Washington, D.C., to raise awareness about overpopulation.

Confront the Opposition

Conflict makes news. Aware of this, some activists deliberately confront their opponents in a public place. Some manipulate news coverage of a large event by creating a conflict. An organization may draw thousands of people to a rally only to have the media focus on a debate or disturbance among a small group of people. The small debate is seen as a good photo opportunity by some journalists because it depicts "both sides" of the issue. (This trick is underhanded, and I don't recommend it under normal circumstances. If you see this kind of conflict happening at an event you've organized, tell the reporters who may rush to cover it that it does not represent your event at all.)

For example, a small number of antiabortion protesters have attended large pro-choice rallies, creating a confrontation and landing a "pro-and-anti-choice face-off" photo in the newspaper. (A photo with "both sides" can appeal to editors.)

Put It in a Trash Can

Activists opposing the full gamut of ills can use a trash can to make their points. Frequently, activists want the object of their campaign (a bill, law, court decision) to be "thrown out." Or an unsafe product should be "trashed."

In the Dumpster.   A coalition of nonprofit groups, including Public Citizen, was trying to make the point that the Multilateral Agreement on Investment would, if approved, "trash" laws relating to labor rights, environmental standards, sovereignty, and sustainable development. Prior to a meeting about the agreement, they rented a dumpster and placed it on the sidewalk in front of the meeting hall. Beside the dumpster, they piled garbage bags clearly labeled "Labor Rights," "Environmental Standards," and so on. Then, after brief comments from a podium about the Multilateral Agreement on Investment, they dumped the trash bags into the dumpster. A pack of photographers documented the event.

Tobacco and the Tax Code.   In a symbolic reenactment of history, tobacco farmers threw out bales of tobacco to protest proposed taxes, and members of Congress dumped the federal tax code into Boston Harbor on April 15, tax day.

TV Trash. To illustrate that television is full of trash, antitelevision activists did the obvious. They threw a television set in a trash can.

Create a Spectacle

Journalists have an eye out for the unusual, and sometimes simply creating a spectacle at the right time can generate coverage. I can't tell you when a "spectacle" goes too far from the media's perspective. But here are some examples to help you make your own decision.

Exorcism of the Pentagon. During the Vietnam War, Abbie Hoffman hatched the idea of surrounding the Pentagon and, as part of a religious ceremony, exorcising its evil. The police refused to let the hippies encircle the Pentagon, and Hoffman didn't have enough people to do it anyway. But the media event proceeded with the hippies chanting into an amplification system (as quoted in Marty Jezer's book *Abbie Hoffman, American Rebel*): "In the name of the generative power of Priapus, in the name of the totality, we call upon the demons of the Pentagon to rid themselves of the cancerous tumors of the war generals." The plan created quite a bit of media hype and to this day is one of the best-known hippie stunts of the 1960s. But according to Jezer's book, it was actually a tiny part of a 50,000-person march on the Lincoln Memorial. (Hoffman was a spectacle master, by his own admission more concerned with visual presentation than factual analysis. He was the one who illustrated the greed of Wall Street by throwing dollar bills from the visitors' gallery of the New York Stock Exchange and watching the traders dive for them. In a lesser-known protest opposing traffic in New York City, he orga-

nized a "do-your-own-thing" event, temporarily shutting down
St. Marks Place with dancing hippies.)

Burning the Puppy. In his book *How You Can Manipulate the Media*, David Alexander describes an incident in which a man announced to the news media that he was going to pour gasoline on
a puppy and burn it at a news conference. Newspapers ran stories about his plans, and of course citizens were outraged. The
police could do nothing because it's not a crime to threaten to kill
a puppy. At the scheduled news conference, a man emerged with
a puppy in his arms. With live cameras rolling (it was the 5 P.M.
news hour), he criticized journalists for caring more about pup-
pies than people and expressed outrage at U.S. foreign policy in
Central America. He said he would not burn the puppy after all.

Climb a Tree, Kiss a Pig, and Parachute into a Convention Hall.
When a government agency released a report about a toxic site,
an activist climbed a tree and talked to reporters on a cellular
phone. Principal Don Bruno of Cotton Creek Elementary School
in Westminster, Colorado, generated a minimedia event when he
kissed a pot-bellied pig as a payoff for students meeting his challenge to read 140,000 minutes in February. Activists have para-
chuted into conventions and other outdoor events.

Encircle a Target

It's worth thinking long and hard before organizing a traditional
march or rally. Journalists look at these honorable means of democratic expression as boring. You might ask yourself, How can we
involve a large group of people in our "rally" yet not have a
rally? One way is to encircle something, perhaps a building, a
statue, anything that might be relevant to your issue. You don't
even have to use people to encircle you target. Ribbons, tape, or
other objects might do the trick.

A Human Chain. Activists in Boulder, Colorado, repeatedly tried to form a human chain around the ten-square-mile Rocky Flats nuclear-bomb plant. Each time they undertook the protest, they received substantial media coverage, though some reporters emphasized their failure to accomplish the encirclement rather than their point that the plant should be closed. Nonetheless, photographs of segments of the encirclement, with people holding hands in front of the fenced, austere bomb plant, were irresistible to TV and print photographers.

Circles of Banned Books or of Human Replicas. Students listed the titles of banned books on separate pieces of paper and linked them together to form a paper chain used to encircle the library during Banned Books Week. An activist encircled fifteen waste barrels assembled on the Colorado capitol lawn with life-sized human figures, which were created by school kids, artists, and activists to represent themselves at the event.

Present Your Organization in Action

Often, you don't need to stage anything for reporters. Simply let them know when your organization is doing something interesting, particularly if it has visual appeal. Every day, nonprofit groups are doing interesting things, but too frequently staff and volunteers forget about letting the news media know. Depending on how busy journalists are on a given day, almost any community activity—even a meeting—can make news. If you want feature-length coverage of an event or program—not just a photograph in the news—you'll have to contact feature writers well in advance. (See Chapter 18, "Pitch a Feature Story.")

Police Arrest Suspected Prostitutes. It appeared that the front-page newspaper photo and television news video of a police officer arresting a suspected prostitute was the result of photographers just happening to be in the right place at the right time—or listening to the police radio. But luck had nothing to do with it. Knowing that the opportunity to photograph prostitutes being apprehended by police could be attractive to news outlets, the police department invited journalists to accompany officers on a sting operation, which resulted in thirteen arrests.

Boy Scouts, Kids, Churches, and More.   Boy Scouts practice survival skills in a mock disaster. A day-care class goes to the park on "kite day." A church group removes graffiti from underpasses. An environmental group meets with Russian officials.

Link Your Event to a Season or Holiday

Reporters are constantly looking for new ways to cover the holidays or seasonal changes. From a journalist's perspective, the holidays *have* to be covered. Yet the same old stuff doesn't grab people. Take advantage of this by offering journalists something different to cover.

Antiabortion Haunted House.   Antiabortion activists in Denver made national news with their "haunted house" around Halloween. The "horrors" in the house, located at a church, included bloody "abortions," drug-addicted teens, and other symbols of the right-wing political agenda. The haunted house was denounced by pro-choice activists, which propelled the story further in the media.

Memorial Day, Valentine's Day, and Prom Night.   The surgeon general's recommendations on drunk driving were released around Memorial Day to take advantage of journalists' interest in drunk driving during that weekend. Valentine's Day was used by Planned Parenthood to offer discounts on vasectomies. Groups concerned about teenage drunk driving have used the prom season to inject their concerns in the news.

Write Simple Reports

Reports released by government, nonprofit organizations, and academics have facts and figures that journalists want. Lengthy reports with credible data frequently make news, but so do easy-to-write reports with anecdotal information. You can devise a creative "report" that could make news, particularly if it's released when your issue is in the news. (See Chapter 29, "Publicize a Report or Academic Paper.")

Beer or Presidents. The Center for Science in the Public Interest in Washington, D.C., focuses on health issues. It often releases detailed reports analyzing the fat content of foods. In a simple study, however, the organization surveyed just a few fourth-grade classes near Washington, D.C. *Media Advocacy and Public Health* tells how the center asked students to name U.S. presidents and brands of beer. The fourth-graders could not only name more brands of beer than presidents but were more likely to spell the beer brands correctly. These findings received wide coverage—as did a much more expensive and complex academic study revealing that children were as likely to identify Joe Camel (the cartoon figure on Camel cigarettes) as they were Mickey Mouse!

Raise Money for an Alternative

A bake sale isn't news. But if you're having one to raise money to pay off the national deficit, it can be. A self-mocking fund-raiser like this can be newsworthy.

When I was a college student, the Brown Disarmament Group opposed decisions by professors to accept Defense Department grants to help devise Star Wars, the space-based missile system. Professors responded to our opposition by claiming that they could not fund their research, which had civilian applications, any other way. To illustrate the predicament, our group staged a bake sale to raise money to replace a Brown professor's Star Wars grant. We hoped that the media coverage of the bake sale might inspire some rich person to dump a pile of money on us. Unfortunately, it didn't, and we raised a total of $63, but we made news and made people think.

Also consider these media events:

Painting a mural
Celebrating or parading
Rallying for what you *don't* want (mutants for nuclear power)
Altering or co-opting your opponent's symbol or sign
Marking an anniversary
Burning something
Offering a reward
Fasting
Boycotting
Promising or pledging to do something
Handing out something unusual
Sponsoring a contest or art show
Run-athoning, dance-athoning, skate-athoning, or any-athoning

Tips for Creating a Good Photo Opportunity

As you set up your media event, think about how photographers will view it. "Think about how it will look in the newspaper and on the TV screen," says Tim Brakemeier, a photographer for the German Press Agency, a news service in Germany.

- Note the background. Make sure that it's not distracting, or better yet, select a background that's relevant to your event and message.

- Outside is generally better than inside. "Outside, the sun can be a problem; so can noise, weather, and street people," says Jeffrey Scharig, a photographer for Reuters, a news service.
- Try to have the sun shining on the objects you want photographed. Sidelighting is the biggest headache for photographers; backlighting is second best.
- Make sure signs or banners are readable from a distance.
- Don't leave items lying around that you don't want photographed. "On my hunger strike, I told reporters I was drinking juice, so it wasn't a secret," says environmental activist Tim Ream of Portland, Oregon. "But the natural inclination for photographers was to shoot the juice bottles I had. So I put them aside."
- Consider putting your banner message on your clothes in case your signs and banners are removed or cropped from the photo.
- Remember, photographers like action shots—not set-up arrangements. But if you see photographers, turn your signs in their direction.
- Create your event so a photographer has few (or no!) options to take photographs that you would rather *not* see in the news.

5

Choose a Time
to Maximize Coverage

Y<small>OU CAN'T STOP THE GAS LINE</small> under Sweetkids Elementary
from exploding—setting fire to hundreds of Halloween lunch
boxes and eclipsing the press conference you are holding at the
same time. But staging your event on certain days at certain times
will increase your chances of being covered.

For Best Coverage, Monday Through Thursday

Reporters generally work long but regular hours. Both broadcast
and print media pare down their staffs substantially on week-
ends and after deadlines on weekdays, leaving only a couple of
reporters in the newsroom instead of dozens. Barring exceptions
(read on) it's best to stage your event Monday through Thursday
between 10 A.M. and 2 P.M.

Because of traffic and deadlines, an event after 3 P.M. is a
headache for most reporters. Only the most newsworthy events
will be covered in the late afternoon or evening. "Timing is everything," says Tom Donahue, Miami bureau chief for CBS News.
"They might have something real interesting to say, but if they
have a press conference at 6 P.M., we can't do much with it."

If your event is powerful and relevant enough, it will be covered no matter when you hold it and regardless of routine dead-

lines. But only rarely, if ever, will your event fall into the must-be-covered-no-matter-what category.

If you're tailoring your event for local TV news and it's got excellent visual components, stage it at 5 P.M. or 10 P.M., allowing local TV news to broadcast live at the scene. If you hold a weekend event, Saturday afternoon is a terrible time for print media because the first editions of Sunday's paper are out Saturday morning. If you want to hold an event on the weekend, stage it on Sunday for coverage on TV Sunday night and in Monday's newspaper. Sunday can be a slow news day, increasing your odds of being covered.

Staging an event on Friday is not a good idea because Saturday's paper usually has fewer pages, so there is less space for news; and many reporters are busy on Friday writing for Sunday's paper. Also, fewer people read Saturday's paper or watch the evening news on Friday night.

In fact, Friday is such a loser that Steve Chavis, former news director of Denver's KBCO-FM radio, said, "I'm surprised people ever hold press events on Friday."

For Photographs,
Try Monday, Tuesday, or Sunday Morning

Newspaper photographers are least busy Monday and Tuesday after 10 A.M. Wednesday and Thursday are busier because photographers are shooting for Sunday's paper. Friday is a bad day because Saturday's paper contains fewer photos. Weekdays prior to a holiday can also be hectic for photographers and writers alike.

Sunday morning, before the afternoon sports trauma, can be an excellent time because photographers are looking for shots for Monday's paper and there's generally not a lot happening. (Notice how many shots of running races appear in Monday's paper.)

A photo that's taken in the evening—if it sees the light of day at all—will almost certainly be black and white. (See Chapter 23, "Influence Newspaper Photographers.")

Dodge Busy News Days and the "Sweeps"

The slower the news day, the better your chances of being covered. Logically, then, you want to avoid days when you know a major media event is scheduled (e.g., Super Bowls, court trials, elections).

Nielsen periodically rates television programs based on how many viewers they attract. (Arbitron rates radio programs.) The stakes are enormous: Programs with higher ratings charge higher advertising rates. Networks respond to the "sweeps," as the ratings are called, by running extra promotions.

For television news, the sweeps month translates into maximum blood, supreme pathos, and consummate sentimentality. You'll hear the stations promoting—with extra gusto—upcoming television news segments. Some of these segments have been weeks or months in the making.

It can be hard for cause-related events to compete. Don't be "swept" under the rug. Find out when the sweeps happen and avoid them.

React Quickly to Breaking News

Try to determine if your event is strong enough to stand on its own or if it needs to ride the coattails of another media event. (See Chapter 3, "Determine What's Newsworthy.") If you've got Dustin Hoffman leading a caravan of 20,000 farmers in tractors to the state capitol, you can pick your time and date. If all you've got is three activists in penguin suits and you're trying to draw attention to the slaughter of penguins, you'd better wait until something related to penguin killing is already in the news.

Put two activists together and instead of *doing* something, they'll form two committees. While the committees are meeting, opportunities for coverage are lost and the cause suffers.

You have to speak to the media when they are available. It's best to anticipate in advance when an opportunity for coverage will arise and to be prepared.

If a major story has broken in the national news media about your cause—or there is an ongoing national debate about it—local news outlets may be looking for "local angles" about the story, making your event more newsworthy. (See "Tips for Reacting to Breaking News" in Chapter 17, "Suggest Ideas for News Stories to Journalists.")

Similarly, if a major story has broken in the local news media about your cause and the media have not heard from community groups—or even citizens representing a different perspective on a given issue—your event may well be a hit. But you've got to act fast—preferably no later than the day after the news breaks. The more time that elapses between the major news event and your response, the less coverage you can expect to receive. However, if six months or more passes during which there has been no local media coverage of your cause—and your issue is still relevant—the media may see your event as an opportunity to update readers on your issue.

If citizens have already staged an event in response to a development related to your cause, it is far less likely that your follow-up event will receive much coverage. This is particularly true if "your side's" response was already reported.

Be Flexible

Alter your plans if developments in the news dictate that you do so. For example, when I was working for Greenpeace, I planned for months to release a report in Ft. Lauderdale, Florida, exposing that Florida would be among the top pollution-generating states in the United States by 2012. The report described how Florida's pollution from coal-fired power plants could be contributing to global warming, which could cause catastrophic climatic changes worldwide. The report outlined anecdotal evidence that impacts of global warming—including droughts, floods, hurricanes, and temperature increases—were already detectable worldwide.

We planned to deliver our report in a coffin to a major power company near Miami. I flew to Florida on Monday, and just hours after the plane landed, an unseasonal tropical storm named Gordon hit. Our plan to release our report Thursday no longer seemed viable because all the major news media were fixated on the storm, which was causing serious damage. The news media were particularly obsessed with the saga of a giant barge that had become stranded right off the beach.

We changed our plans, deciding that raising a possible link between the storm and global warming was not only legitimate but consistent with our point. Instead of delivering the report in a coffin to the power company, which was a fairly dubious event in the first place, we placed a banner over the coffin—"Gordon = Early Warning of Global Warming?"—and dragged it to the beach where the barge was stuck. This worked. Our coffin was greeted by local TV news cameras and print and radio reporters. The storm was our news peg, and suddenly global warming, a complex problem that's difficult for the mainstream media to cover, was news. If we had waited for the storm to pass and proceeded with our original plans to deliver the report to the power company, we'd have been lucky to have attracted any media attention at all, especially on Miami local TV news, which is known for its thirst for mayhem.

Sample Timetable for
Organizing a Media Event

Here's a five-month timetable for media work leading up to an event. You don't need five months. In fact, with one day's notice, I've organized stunts related to political issues that have received national press coverage. Other types of events—theater productions, art shows, and the like—require many months of advance planning. In any case, the earlier you get started with publicity, the better your chances of letting the world know about your event.

(Details about how to execute the following activities below are all described in detail in the other Part 1 chapters of this book.)

Five Months in Advance. Clarify your goals, target audience, and message. If you're organizing an event, settle on an appropriate visual image. Select a location. Obtain a permit, if necessary. Compile a media list, which you should augment as your media outreach proceeds.

Four Months in Advance. Write and distribute a "calendar item" for monthly magazines and other outlets that need to be notified long in advance. Send a press kit, including feature ideas, and follow up with a phone call. Begin your outreach to media sponsors if appropriate.

Two Months in Advance. If you're planning a cultural or art event, arrange for the artists to perform somewhere for free—at a school or senior center—during the week prior to the show's opening. This offers the media another way to cover an art show as news.

Six Weeks in Advance. Distribute a "guest availability" to talk radio and television talk shows. Follow up with phone calls. Make sure all spokespeople are prepared for interviews. They should practice delivering sound bites and answering questions.

One Month in Advance. Distribute your "calendar item" to daily and weekly news outlets and newsletters. Make sure you've got the calendar editor's name right and make follow-up calls to make sure your item is received. Include photos or art for publication in calendars. Call feature writers at daily newspapers with story ideas.

Two Weeks in Advance. If your artists are performing at a pro bono event, distribute a press release about the performance to daily news outlets two days before the pro bono event occurs. Highlight anything unique or highly visual in your press release. Make follow-up calls two days before the performance.

One Week in Advance.   Write your news release for daily newspapers, television news shows, and other daily outlets.

Three Days in Advance.   Distribute your release and follow up with phone calls. Assemble a press kit for the event.

One Day in Advance.   Call all daily news outlets and critics.

Day of the Event.   Place a reminder call to TV stations and journalists who told you they plan to attend. At the event, distribute media kits and assign one or two people to sign in journalists and help them obtain any information they need.

6

Find an
Effective Location

THE LOCATION OF YOUR MEDIA EVENT should provide an image that helps communicate the message you are sending. For example, if you are denouncing a local developer, you should probably stage your event in front of the developer's offices (or the site of a particular development) with the company's sign and logo and *yours* as a backdrop. (For extra conflict, tape a sign with your message over your opponent's sign.) An on-location press conference makes much better sense than holing up in a nondescript room somewhere. It adds a sense of action—even if you are simply holding an otherwise boring press conference. Other factors, however, may weigh against your staging an event at the developer's office. Ask yourself these questions:

Is the Location Convenient?   Most news organizations are understaffed, and reporters are extremely busy. On top of that, many are lazy. Select a location that is close to the downtown area. An artist I know once spent months creating a replica of the deadly plutonium contained in U.S. nuclear bombs. It was an extraordinary visual. But she displayed it in an obscure plaza about an hour away from the nearest news outlet. Since the "exhibit" was definitely not on any reporter's "must cover" list and the location was inconvenient, she received little media coverage.

The news media will come to you wherever you are if you've got a story they want badly enough. The problem is, you'll seldom have such a story. So you should pick a location that's easy for journalists to access.

Is Your Site Commonly Used for Media Events? Most cities have a spot that's well-known to journalists as the Place of the Protesters. Usually it's the state capitol steps. Avoid this location if possible.

If Your Event Is Outdoors, Do You Have a Backup Location? It's always better to hold a press conference outside, and more often than not a little rain or bad weather won't hurt your chances of being covered. But you should have backup plans in case severe weather strikes. It could be best to reschedule your event, as stories about severe weather may cut deeply into TV news.

Do You Need a Permit? For most events on private property, permits are not required. For public property, permit requirements vary substantially from municipality to municipality. Generally, sidewalks are less regulated than parks and city squares. If you do not obstruct the sidewalk (i.e., people can walk around you and your props on the sidewalk), a permit is not usually needed, although some cities demand a permit if you are going to place anything on the sidewalk. For larger public spaces (parks, the capitol steps, etc.), a permit is usually required for any demonstration.

Often you will be asked to provide proof of insurance or, if you have none, to buy insurance for your event. You should be able to convince permit offices to waive this requirement if your event is related to politics and therefore protected by the First Amendment. It helps, of course, if you are not selling anything, including food, at your event.

What About Staging an Event Without a Permit? If you stage an event on public property without a permit, you won't be breaking the law until the police ask you to leave. Thus it's possible to complete your event before you're told to move. If asked, you can leave and not be arrested. Also, with the media present, the police may choose not to bother you.

If you set up on private property without permission, you can be charged with trespassing. But again, usually you will first be asked to leave voluntarily.

Where Do You Obtain Permits? For sidewalks, the local police department is usually the place to go. Or start your run through the bureaucracy by calling the county clerk. For parks and city squares, call the city parks department, the maintenance office for the capitol, or possibly the city manager's office.

If you request permits repeatedly, make friends with the workers in the permit office. Sending them a thank-you letter is helpful, as is making sure you clean the site carefully before you leave.

Sample Permit Application

File with: Capitol Complex
                              Attn. Permit Manager

Date of Application _____
Date of Event Scheduled _____   Time _____

Name of Organization Holding Event _____
Contact Person _____ Phone_____
Address _____
Please provide a detailed description of the event, including sales, use of tables, structures, tents, and so on. Attach additional pages as necessary.

Attach proof of insurance in the amount of $500,000 showing that your organization is insured against personal injury or property damage. (Requests are considered for waiver of this provision.)

I have read all attached rules and regulations on the reverse side of this application and agree to comply with all requirements. I further agree to hold the government harmless for any injury resulting from the use of the property.

Waiver of insurance requested_____

Waiver of $100 damage deposit requested _____

_____
Signature   Date

7

Sign Up a
Media Sponsor

IF YOU HAVE THE RIGHT EVENT, try to convince a media organization to "sponsor" it. A media sponsor can be a tremendous help: advertising your event, covering it live, selling tickets, printing programs, and more. Entertainment-oriented and non-controversial events—a run for hunger, kids' day at the zoo, an arts festival, a concert—are most likely to attract sponsors. In exchange, you need to offer your media sponsor something: space for your sponsor's banner at your event, free passes to your event, its logo printed in your event's program or on tickets, time for a spokesperson representing your sponsor to say a few words at your event, and more.

Sponsorship agreements can vary tremendously, from simple to complicated. "I may just send my van out with hula hoops," says Michelle Dirks, director of marketing and promotions for WJMK-FM, a radio station in Chicago.

Most news organizations shy away from sponsoring political events because they don't want to offend any of their viewers, listeners, or readers. Some radio stations, however, may sponsor an event with a political message if their audience (or "market share") is likely to support it. Because there are dozens of radio stations in most media markets (versus only a handful of TV stations), their audiences are highly specific; thus they don't have to try to appeal to everyone. For example, a local radio station in Denver whose listeners are mostly liberal college students and yuppies sent its van to a Planned Parenthood Valentine's Day event involving the free distribution of condoms to passersby.

Key to landing a media sponsor is offering an event its audience will appreciate. "Do I want to be involved with an all-night bike-a-thon?" asks Michelle Dirks at WJMK-FM. "My listeners have kids. They have to be up at six in the morning. I know that my listeners aren't going to be passionate about certain things."

Keep in mind that most media organizations sponsor events for business reasons—not out of the goodness of their hearts. Think about how your event might boost their marketing strategy. "We compare information from organizations with our current marketing strategy," says Angie Clark, community relations manager for the *St. Louis Post-Dispatch*. "Based on our strategy at the time, we evaluate the event."

Tips for Hooking a Media Sponsor

- Try to make your event known around town before you seek media sponsors. An event that's already generating attention will be more attractive to sponsors.
- Zero in on who will attend your event. Then approach media outlets that serve this group of people. For example, if your event will be attended by teenagers, approach teen radio stations for sponsorships.
- Prepare a short proposal (one or two pages) for potential sponsors, describing your event, its history, and who will attend it.
- In your written proposal, be clear on what the media outlet will get from you and what you want in return. Request a meeting to talk about it.
- To gauge interest, send simultaneous sponsorship proposals to different media outlets. Then you can decide which

offer is best for you. However, it's *not* a good idea to pit one media outlet against another in a bidding war.

- You may want to offer a sponsor the "first opportunity" to accept your proposal before you shop around.
- If possible, send sponsorship proposals to outlets at least two months in advance. Address them *by name* to the promotions director or other appropriate person. You'll find that potential sponsors put different staff with different titles in charge of promotions. Find out the correct name and title at the media organization that you are targeting. "If it's a contest that might help build circulation, it would fall under consumer communications," says Angie Clark at the *St. Louis Post-Dispatch*. "If it's cause related or good will, it would fall under community relations."
- You may be able to ask an outlet to provide refreshments, which it might be able to obtain from an advertiser.
- Consider offering the potential sponsor the right to sell banner space, which it can connect to advertising sales.
- If it's OK with your sponsors, sign up multiple sponsors for one event. A sponsor may request that no competitive media (e.g., another TV station) be allowed to sponsor the event.
- If you plan to sell tickets to your event in advance, you can offer your media sponsor the right to sell them. Your sponsor, in turn, can sell a retail store the rights to sell the advance tickets. (This is what's happening when you hear on the radio that tickets to an event are on sale at, say, a record store.)
- Make the event fun for journalists who come. Invite their kids and have food.
- Most community groups have the best luck with radio stations. For smaller events, it's best to determine who will attend and which news media they consume. Television stations generally sponsor only major events.

8

Compile a
Media List

Y ou need to assemble a list of journalists who might be interested in covering your cause. Once your list is in place, you
can access it when you want to distribute a press release or call a
reporter to suggest a news story. With all your media contacts
listed in one location, contacting journalists can be done more ef-
ficiently and quickly.

There's no single correct way to organize a media list. In fact,
what I present in this chapter is probably more elaborate than a
small community group needs. But I hope to inspire you to
gather as much information as possible about news outlets and
journalists. This will pay off for you and your organization in the
long run.

The media list of many nonprofits consists of one sheet of paper listing the dozen or so major media in their area, including
three or four TV stations, one or two daily newspapers, one alternative weekly newspaper, two to four radio news programs, and
a handful of talk-radio shows.

Each news outlet usually has one contact name, fax number,
phone number, and—if available—an e-mail address. The contacts for TV stations are usually assignment editors. For newspapers and news radio, they're reporters. For talk radio, they're producers. The following is a sample skeletal media list entry:

Name of News Outlet	Orlando Sentinel
First Name of Journalist	Katey
Last Name of Journalist	Forell
Title of Journalist	Business Reporter
Phone Number	302-222-3434
Fax Number	302-222-3535
E-Mail Address	kforell@cnn.com

A media list with this basic information will work for many community organizations, particularly if they've made a strategic decision *not* to make media outreach much of a priority. Such a list with a dozen or so entries will allow an organization to do a respectable job of reaching out to the local news media, especially if other tips in this book (e.g., respect deadlines, follow up a news release with a phone call) are mastered.

But a skeletal media list will not allow nonprofits to excel at media outreach and *long-term communications*—reaching the maximum number of people with your message and affecting how they perceive your organization and issues.

A bare-bones list can be disastrous for an organization when staff depart, taking along all the undocumented information in their heads. Make a serious, long-term commitment to getting the word out. Take extra time to create a stellar media list with detailed information.

How to Develop a Media List

Calling citizen groups that work on a cause similar to yours and asking for their media list is the best way to begin. You can take what they've done and build on it; any media list can be improved. If you can't get help from another organization, check the library. There are plenty of reference books, and you'll probably find that a list has already been published. (See Chapter 39, "Sources for Lists of News Outlets.")

Over time, you'll develop relationships with journalists. These contacts will be of the most value in the long run. However, you don't need personal contacts in the media to be an effective publicist. Just act professionally, learn the simple tips in this book, and you will do well.

Keep your media list current. You should update it thoroughly every six months by calling each news outlet to make sure personnel have not changed. Make changes that you note in your day-to-day work as soon as possible. Then if you have to act quickly, you needn't scramble to make sure your information is accurate.

Maintain a list that matches your needs and your computer power. It's useful to have a software program that can retrieve your media data sorted according to any of the categories you set up, as described next. Those lagging behind in the technology race—whether by choice or not—can use a binder with pages that can be changed easily.

How to Organize a Media List

I divide my media list first by *media market* and second by *categories of news outlets* in each market. This way, I can target major metropolitan areas (e.g., the San Francisco market) across the country and have detailed information on the news outlets within those areas.

A media market can be defined as a geographic area with its own television stations and is named after the largest city or cities in it.[1] The broadcasting area of a TV station may extend to a few cities. For example, Minneapolis and St. Paul are in a single media market. So are Seattle and Tacoma and Tampa, St. Petersburg, and Sarasota. One media market may have numerous radio stations, daily newspapers, and other media. In addition, some newspapers or radio stations reach more than one media market. For example, a newspaper may be distributed to an entire state, and there may be multiple television markets within one state.

Each media market has different numbers of news outlets. Usually, however, a market has at least one news outlet from each of these major categories: (1) daily newspapers, (2) weekly newspapers or magazines, (3) quarterly, monthly, or fortnightly newspapers or magazines, (4) daily television news, (5) television public affairs programs, including national TV talk shows and television "news magazines," (6) news radio, (7) talk radio, (8) pop radio, (9) news services, and (10) freelance journalists.

Keep your entries standardized so that groups of news outlets can be retrieved from your list. If you're promoting your event or cause in more than one media market, develop separate lists of outlets for each. If you are a local community organizer in, say, Portland, the bulk of the news outlets on your list will be located in one media market (e.g., the Portland TV-viewing environs).The rest of your list should contain specific information on each news outlet. Following are two sample list entries:

Sample Television News Media List Entry

Market	New York City
Type of News Outlet	daily television news
Name or Call Letters of News Outlet	WNYW TV FOX
Channel	5
First Name of Journalist	Jane
Last Name of Journalist	Reporter
Title	Assignment Editor
Street Address	1234 Broadway
City	New York
State	NY
Zip	10012
Phone	212-222-2222
FAX	212-222-3333
E-Mail	Jay@wnyw.com
Deadline	3:30 P.M.

Format   Live anchors, mostly taped stories
Comments   Typical local news show
History   2/97 Called expressing interest in any
                rallies against media sensationalism.
                7/97 Receptive to our throw-the-TV-in-the-
                dumpster event, but did not send crew.

Sample Print Media List Entry

Market	Los Angeles and National
Type of News Outlet	daily newspaper
Name or Call Letters of News Outlet	*Los Angeles Times*
Channel	
First Name of Journalist	Jay
Last Name of Journalist	Reporter
Title	Media Critic
Street Address	Times Mirror Square
City	Los Angeles
State	CA
Zip	90053
Phone	213-237-7000
FAX	213-237-7968
E-Mail	Jay@latimes.com
Deadline	3:30 P.M.
Format	Major metropolitan daily, plus national coverage
Comments	Very unreceptive to media literacy report 4/97.
History	Called for a comment on citizen access to editorial pages 8/97. Wrote an excellent piece on 2/1/98.

After the name or call letters of a news outlet, make sure you specify AM or FM for radio. Also, note the power of the signal. Fifty-thousand-watt stations and above can cover a whole state, whereas 2,000-watt stations have weak signals that carry only a few miles.

Keep journalist titles standardized so you can retrieve them together if need be. You could use the standard titles used by news outlets. Be as specific as possible. For example, don't just use the title "reporter." Specify what kind, such as "business reporter." Here are some common titles appearing in my media list: assignment editor, anchor, general reporter, environment reporter, editorial page editor, cartoonist, columnist, photo editor, news director, community calendar editor, talk-show host, and producer. See the next section for complete lists of typical titles at news outlets.

In the format section for radio and TV, describe the number of guests, whether the show is live or taped, whether calls are accepted, and so on.

The comments section is useful for recording anything unusual about the outlet. Is this a specialty, alternative, or industry outlet? For broadcast outlets, describe the slant of the show, including the personality of the host, if applicable, and the typical topics.

To provide your group with "media memory," record in the history section all coverage your organization receives from each outlet, including instances when a reporter calls you and how you were treated. This may be too much to do thoroughly in the heat of day-to-day work, but it's worth a try, particularly if a noteworthy media interaction takes place.

Whom to Contact at News Outlets

As you interact with journalists and other media professionals (and expand your media list), you will develop a professional— not necessarily friendly—relationship with them. This will add immeasurably to your ability to garner media attention. (See Chapter

34, "Cultivate Relationships with Journalists.") Here is a description of the type of staff who should be your point of contact at each news outlet. (Also see Chapter 30, "Make National News.")

Daily Newspapers

Your best contacts are reporters, photographers, and editorial page staff. Your media list should include names of reporters, photographers, news editors, calendar editors, editorial writers, columnists, and cartoonists.

If you are trying to generate coverage of a news event, contact reporters. Reporters generally make decisions about whether a story is newsworthy. Editors assign stories as well, but at most local or national dailies, "beat" reporters make most of the decisions—perhaps after checking briefly with an editor. (Beat reporters cover issue areas, for example, education, environment, police.) If the paper is too small to have beat reporters, contact the city editor or editor. If your story does not relate to a particular beat, you should contact an editor unless you have a good relationship with a general assignment reporter. "If a reporter's too busy, he might toss [your story], but an editor might have another reporter available to cover it," says Jack Broom, a reporter for the *Seattle Times*.

You can help out the photo department—and your cause—by sending a release about your event directly to photo editors as well as to the appropriate reporter or news editor. At newspapers, unlike at television stations, reporters do not necessarily consider the visual aspects of a story to be all that important. As a result, reporters and editors often leave photographers in the dark, depriving them of the opportunity to shoot the exquisite visual prop you've created for your event.

"It's probably best to have us both clued into it," says *Boulder Daily Camera* photographer Cliff Grassmick. Address your release to the photo assignment editor or, at smaller papers, the photo editor. (See Chapter 23, "Influence Newspaper Photographers"; for information about how to contact columnists, editorial writers, calendar editors, and columnists, see Part 2, "How to Generate News Coverage Without Staging a Media Event.")

Weekly or Monthly Publications

Your best contacts are freelance journalists or reporters. Most monthlies rely heavily on freelance journalists, making them your point of contact. (Freelance journalists sell their work on a piece-by-piece basis. They usually work for numerous outlets, but most often they sell their work regularly to a handful of outlets. If a freelancer is associated regularly with one outlet, you may want to list him or her under the name of that outlet in your media list.)

At weeklies, you should call reporters or the editor. Remember that most weeklies and monthlies do not cover day-to-day events or breaking news, but they do cover many important issues in a more in-depth fashion. Don't ignore free weeklies just because they appear to be "alternative." Such publications are widely read.

Local Television News

Your best contacts are assignment editors. They are the point of contact at most local television stations. (At some stations, the planning editor should receive news releases.) As always, it's best to address a news release to a specific assignment editor.

Decisions about covering a day's events are usually made at a morning meeting of staff and reporters. Of course, a breaking story radically affects what dominates the limited news time on TV, just as it will alter the front page—but not all the pages—of a newspaper.

Local TV news has a small news "hole"—typically about one-third of the thirty-five-minute show. (Most of the remaining time is spent on weather, sports, and, of course, commercials.) Most of the local TV news hole is filled with stories of disaster and crime. As a result, it's hard to capture the attention of local TV news.

National Television News

Your best contacts are producers. The national network daily news shows have larger news holes than local news shows, but it's more difficult to attract them to any cause. To try, contact a producer by name. It can be hard to get through to national network reporters and producers, but it could be worth it if you've got the time and the right story.

Cable News Network (CNN) has around-the-clock news programming and a huge news hole and is often interested in timely events by citizens. Its audience is smaller than the network news programs but represents the public policy crowd (politicians, their staffs, concerned citizens, journalists), which you may want to reach. CNN is a fixture in many newspaper newsrooms around the world. (Remember, Saddam Hussein watched CNN to orchestrate his response to U.S. action and policies at the time of the Gulf War.) Don't forget other national cable news networks: Fox, CNBC, MSNBC, CNN International. C-SPAN covers conferences, hearings, and lectures of national interest. The future will bring more cable networks. (For more information on cable television, see Chapter 26, "Place Your TV Production or Information on Cable.")

TV Public Affairs Programs, National TV Talk Shows, and TV News Magazines

Your best contacts are producers of specific shows you are targeting. These programs might plan shows on issues months in advance, and they might want your perspective. When you call, make sure you identify a producer by name.

News Radio

Your best contacts are reporters or news directors. A typical media market may have only a couple of radio stations that have news departments with reporters. In most cases, a sole news director handles all news programming. A radio station broadcasting all news without music or talk-radio programming is a rarity.

Talk Radio and Pop Radio

Your best contacts are producers, hosts, or disc jockeys. For pop radio, contact the disc jockeys. For talk radio, contact the producer or host. (See Chapter 25, "Tune Your Cause to Talk Radio.")

News Services

Your best contacts are news editors and photographers. All kinds of news outlets, including newspapers, radio programs, and television stations, subscribe to news services that provide news stories, photos, video, and other information.

Of the news services, the Associated Press (AP) has the most offices across the United States, including scores of staff writers based in New York and Washington, D.C. Most, if not all, daily news outlets subscribe to AP.

At the state level, the Associated Press "news editor" who's on duty when your news release is received—or when you call—will decide whether your story merits AP coverage. You should contact "the news editor," not a specific person. "In many cases, if we get something with a name on it, it winds up in a mail box," says Bill Schiffmann, a news editor for the AP's San Francisco bureau. "And if someone's on vacation, it may sit there for two weeks."

Unlike major local newspapers, most local AP bureaus don't have reporters assigned to beats or issue areas; they have generalists who cover the most important stories in the state. In Washington, D.C., however, a handful of news editors—with reporters working for them—do cover beats such as foreign news and Capitol Hill. Thus in that city you should contact the news editor who's responsible for coverage of your issue.

If your story is covered by AP, it's likely you'll never see a reporter. AP reporters often don't have time to leave the office. They're literally always on deadline because news outlets in different time zones around the world are always on deadline, and news outlets from all over the world subscribe to AP. AP reporters write short news stories—often of less than a few hundred words. Your skill at simplifying your pitch will pay off. (For more on AP, including tips on how to attract AP to your story, see Chapter 30, "Promote a Story to Journalists at National News Outlets," and Chapter 10, "Distribute a News Release.")

Other news services include Bloomberg Business News, which has a large network of offices covering business stories; States News Services, which offers Washington, D.C., news; Reuters (pronounced roy-ters), which is larger in Europe than in the United States; and United Press International, which has endured deep cuts during the past decade but still has divisions around the United States. Certain national newspapers, such as the *New York Times, Los Angeles Times,* and *Washington Post,* also make stories available to news outlets that subscribe. Some newspaper chains, for example, Gannett News Service, Hearst News Service, Knight-Ridder Newspapers, and Thomson Newspapers, maintain offices in Washington, D.C., and send stories to their networks around the country. There are numerous specialty news services as well, including AlterNet in San Francisco, serving alternative news media; Baptist News Service, serving state Baptist weeklies; Hispanic Link News Service, serving Hispanic-oriented weeklies; and many others. News services such as Creators Syndicate, King Features, and Universal Press Syndicate distribute the work of columnists and feature writers.

Some larger cities have their own local news services—for example, City News in San Francisco and City News Bureau in Chicago—that cover local news and have local subscribers.

There are also news services in foreign countries, such as Jiji Press in Japan or Agence France-Presse in France. If your story has international relevance, check for news services in the countries where you want to receive coverage. Some have offices in the United States.

Use Diverse Media to Your Advantage

One key to publicizing a cause is to take advantage of the diversity of the media. Although the most powerful news media can be very similar (witness network television news), there are other outlets that specifically seek stories that the major media ignore or that serve specific audiences whom you may want to reach. And some small outlets may cater exactly to your target audience. For example, to communicate to a state legislator, you may seek coverage in a neighborhood weekly newspaper rather than a large metropolitan daily.

The fact that fewer people read the newspaper or listen to the radio does not mean you should focus your efforts on TV. The segment of the population that reads the paper may be exactly the one your campaign needs to reach.

9

Write a News Release

A NEWS RELEASE IS the vehicle for alerting the media to your event. It's a brief written explanation of your plans.

"I might have thirty seconds to spend on a news release," says Paul Day, a reporter for KCNC-TV, the CBS affiliate in Denver, adding that he has to be "hit over the head with ideas" and that the important information should "leap off the page."

"When I get to the office in the morning, I already have 20 or so news releases waiting, most of them dull," says Claus Kleber, chief U.S. correspondent for KRD, German public television.

"What it all comes down to is the headline," says Steve Chavis, former news director at KBCO-FM, a Boulder radio station.

Tough standards to meet? Not necessarily. Most news releases are written poorly. With some creativity and basic pointers, your release can stand out from the pile. Also, most news releases come from private companies or individuals promoting products or services. As a promoter of a cause, you have an advantage—in the eyes of a news editor—over your average corporate public relations manager.

Tips for Writing a News Release

- In the top left corner, type "For Immediate Release."
- In the top right corner, type the date.

- Below "For Immediate Release," type names and phone numbers of two contacts. Make sure these contacts can be easily reached by phone.
- Use a larger font for your headline than for the text of the release.
- Type a headline on the release. This can be up to four lines if necessary. Include as much essential information as possible.
- Only unusual circumstances require a release of more than one page. Narrow the margins if necessary to fit more information on one page. Have additional concise information available for reporters and editors.
- Try one sentence per paragraph; at most, use three.
- Write the release like a news story with the information in descending order of importance.
- Spend 75 percent of your time writing the headline and first paragraph.
- Your release should answer who, what, where, when, and how. If you prefer, you can write these words on the left side of the page and answer them on the right side.
- Emphasize what's unique: the first, the biggest, and so on.
- Type "—30—" or "###" at the end of your release. This is how journalists mark the end of news copy.
- Type "MORE" at the end of page 1 if your release is two pages, and put a contact phone number and short headline in the upper-right corner of subsequent pages.
- Type your release on the letterhead of an organization even if a coalition of groups is writing it.
- Don't be afraid to be creative. If you've organized a celebratory event, copy your release on colored paper. You might try black with white letters if you've got some sort of frightening event planned.
- Briefly describe your organization in the last paragraph of your news release.
- The two key points are to keep it short and write a good headline.

Four Sample News Releases

ENVIRONMENTAL WORKING GROUP

CALIFORNIA OFFICE P.O. BOX 29034 SAN FRANCISCO, CA 94129 (415) 561-6598 FAX (415) 561-6480

FOR IMMEDIATE RELEASE: June 13, 1997

CONTACT: Richard Wiles, (202) 667-6982; Bill Walker, (415) 5610-6598

People of Color in California Breathe the Heaviest Pollution --
Air in Minority Communities 3 Times More Likely to be Unhealthy

WASHINGTON -- In California, the more likely you are to live in a community of color, the more likely you are to breathe unhealthy air.

An Environmental Working Group (EWG) analysis found that Californians who live in neighborhoods with a higher than average population of persons of color are nearly three times more likely to be exposed to unsafe levels of particulate pollution than residents of neighborhoods with a higher than average white population. Fifty-four percent of all air pollution monitors in communities of color showed levels of fine particle pollution (PM-2.5) exceeding the U.S. Environmental Protection Agency's proposed health standard, compared to just 19 percent of the monitors in predominantly white communities.

"This is a striking example of the disproportionate impact of pollution on communities of color," said Richard Wiles, EWG's vice president for research and author of the report released today. "On the positive side, it shows that just as people of color are harmed the most by dirty air, they stand to benefit most from new standards for cleaner air. "

The report comes as the EPA prepares next month to submit its final recommendations for the new health standards -- and as major polluters are waging a major disinformation campaign to undermine the EPA proposal.

One strategy being employed by industry front groups such as Citizens for a Sound Economy is to target communities of color with a message that EPA's proposed health standard will place undue financial burdens on black and minority small business owners. In fact, control strategies for particle pollution will be largely directed at large industrial polluters and electric utilities -- none of which qualifies as a minority-owned small business. Large industrial polluters contribute 96 percent of the sulfur dioxide, 56 percent of the direct particulates and 48 percent of the nitrogran oxides that make up PM-2.5.

EWG's analysis of air pollution data from 162 air monitors across the state found that the average annual level of airborne toxic particles in communities of color was 17.2 micrograms per cubic meter of air (ug/m3) -- compared to an average yearly level of 11.7 ug/m3 in predominantly white communities. The EPA's proposed standard is 15 ug/m3. However, the California Air Resources Board has recommended an even tougher standard of 12 ug/m3.

The report classifies California communities of color as all census tracts with a Hispanic, African-American, Asian and/or Native American population greater than 42 percent, which was the statewide proportion of such groups in the 1980 census. Census tracts with less than a 42 percent share of those ethnic groups were classified as predominantly white communities.

The report is available online at www.ewg.org.

A complex report on air pollution is summed up in one simple sentence, which is the lead paragraph of this news release. Note that the full report is available on the Internet. Credit: Environmental Working Group

GREENPEACE
1021 PEARL STREET, SUITE 200
BOULDER, COLORADO 80302
(303) 786-8805   FAX (303) 786-7211

FOR IMMEDIATE RELEASE   January 15, 1992

Contact: Jason Salzman
             (303) 786-8805
             Suzanne Pomeroy
             (303) 440-3381

PORK-BARREL POLITICS: 'PIGS' PROTEST PLUTONIUM PLANS
At Rally Thursday, Activists Say Flats 'Feeding at Public Trough'

BOULDER, Jan. 15 (GP) -- Federal officials testifying Thursday at a key hearing on restarting the Rocky Flats nuclear bomb plant will be confronted with a dramatic demonstration by activists protesting the "wasteful pork-barrel politics of nuclear bomb production."

The activists will be the ones dressed as pigs.

The pigs will lead an anti-nuclear rally beginning a 1:15 p.m. Thursday, January 16, in front of the U.S. Department of Commerce Building, 325 Broadway in Boulder. Inside, a public hearing on the Energy Department's proposal to restart an idle plutonium lab will begin at 1:30 p.m. with testimony by Rocky Flats officials. Public comments are scheduled for 6:30 p.m.

"Rocky Flats officials will probably snort at our rally," says Jason Salzman of Greenpeace. "But that's because they are feeding at the public trough. While some would rake in the bacon, taxpayers would absorb a nuclear first-strike attack if bomb production resumes."

The public hearing in Boulder will focus on the resumption of plutonium operations in Building 559. Department of Energy officials have stated that Building 559 would be used for tasks relating to nuclear weapons production and waste cleanup at Rocky Flats. Groups sponsoring the Boulder rally say they favor safe cleanup of Rocky Flats but oppose all activities related to nuclear weapons production.

Rocky Flats, which produced plutonium triggers for nuclear weapons, has been shut down since November 1989. Despite the end of the Cold War, Rocky Flats officials continue to state that the plant will begin producing triggers again by about April 1.

The Jan. 16 rally is sponsored by Greenpeace, the Rocky Mountain Peace Center, and SANE/Freeze. Greenpeace is an international environmental organization with offices in 35 countries around the world.

-- 30 --

Printed on recycled paper.

If it's appropriate, be creative. News releases that make interesting reading will attract the attention of journalists who see dozens or more each day. Credit: Greenpeace

Amnesty International USA

For Immediate Release
July 16, 1997

News Release

Contact: Lurma Rackley
(202) 544-0200 ext. 230

National Office
322 Eighth Avenue
New York, NY 10001
(212) 807-8400
Fax: (212) 727-3611

Washington Office
304 Pennsylvania Avenue, SE
Washington, DC 20003
(202) 544-0200
Fax: (202) 675-8585

Northeast Regional Office
58 Day Street - Davis Square
Somerville, MA 02144
(617) 623-0202
Fax: (617) 623-2005

Mid-Atlantic Regional Office
1118 22nd Street, NW
Washington, DC 20037
(202) 775-5161
Fax: (202) 775-5992

Southern Regional Office
131 Ponce de Leon Ave, NE #220
Atlanta, GA 30308
(404) 876-5661
Fax: (404) 876-2276

Midwest Regional Office
53 West Jackson - Room 1162
Chicago, IL 60604
(312) 427-2060
Fax: (818) 427-2610

Urgent Action Office
PO Box 1270
Nederland, CO 80466
(303) 440-0913
Fax: (303) 258-7881

Western Regional Office
9000 W. Washington Blvd, 2nd Floor
Culver City, CA 90232
(310) 815-0450
Fax: (310) 815-0457

San Francisco Office
500 Sansome Street, Suite 615
San Francisco, CA 94111
(415) 291-9233
Fax: (415) 291-8722

Refugee Office
500 Sansome Street, Suite 615
San Francisco, CA 94111
(415) 291-0601
Fax: (415) 291-8722

**Three US Companies in Power Plant Venture In India
Must Ensure Human Rights Protections, Amnesty International Says**

Citing reports that Indian state police are heavily suppressing protests against construction of a power plant being built by three US-based multinational corporations, Amnesty International has written to the companies asking them to use their influence to ensure human rights standards are fully respected. Amnesty International USA sent letters today to the companies: Enron of Texas, General Electric Corporation of Connecticut, and Bechtel Incorporated of California.

"We are very concerned about the treatment of villagers and activists protesting against the construction of the Dabhol Power Company plant, a joint venture between the three U.S. multinationals," said Curt Goering, Deputy Executive Director of Amnesty International USA. Several hundred peaceful protesters -- demonstrating against the plant's potential effect on the local population and the environment -- in recent months have been subjected to harassment, arbitrary arrest, ill-treatment and preventive detention under the ordinary criminal law, Amnesty found.

"A battalion of the State Reserve Police, stationed on the site of the power plant, the local police, and company security guards have all been implicated in these violations," Amnesty researchers reported. "Such collusion of the police with those supporting the construction of the power plant has increased the vulnerability of protesters to human rights violations. We consider those arrested and imprisoned simply for peacefully protesting against construction of the power plant to be prisoners of conscience," Amnesty officials declared.

In a report released today, Amnesty International calls on the companies to adopt and enforce a policy on human rights; to ensure that the training of all managers and staff reflects the rights set out in the Universal Declaration of Human Rights; to maintain regular contact with human rights organizations in India, as well as international organizations, so that views can be shared and concerns can be freely discussed; to publicly urge a full and impartial investigation into all reported human rights violations, and urge that the perpetrators be brought to justice; and to establish strict guidelines for all security personnel subcontracted by, seconded to or employed by the DPC, to ensure their training reflects international human rights standards, and to ensure they are fully accountable.

Amnesty International also called on the Government of India and the Maharashtra state government to ensure human rights protections. To receive a copy of the report, "India: Suppression of protests in Maharashtra," call AIUSA at (202) 544-0200 or (212) 633-4251.

Dr. Morton E. Winston, Chair, Board of Directors • Dr. William F. Schulz, Executive Director

Even a news release with lots of details—like this one—should not exceed one page. Credit: Amnesty International USA

88

National Coalition for the Homeless

PRESS RELEASE

For Immediate Release
March 1, 1995

Contact
Fred Karnas, Jr.
Barbara Duffield
202/775-1322

A formerly homeless Harvard student, the 1994 National Teacher of the year, Members of Congress, and advocates gathered outside the U.S. Capitol today to decry the proposed elimination of funding education programs for homeless children and youth.

Last week, the House Appropriations Subcommittee on Labor, Health and Human Services, and Education voted to eliminate all funding for the program. Several hundred thousand homeless children nationwide benefit from the $28.8 million program which provides services to help homeless children and youth enroll, attend, and succeed in school. The full House Appropriations Committee is expected to act this week and the floor vote will take place next week.

Fred Karnas, Jr., executive director of the National Coalition for the Homeless argued that "The proposed cuts are cruel and incredibly short-sighted. Where are the family values advocates when proposals like this put our nation's most vulnerable children in peril?"

Karnas added, "In the short-term, it is the children who will pay the price for these outrageous and unjustifiable cuts, but ultimately we will all be diminished by our failure to ensure that homeless children have the tools they need to climb out of poverty."

Sandra McBrayer, 1994 National Teacher of the Year, passionately described some of the homeless youth who she sees every day in the Homeless Outreach School she founded in San Diego. McBrayer added, "The proposed rescissions are contrary to one of our most basic American values, the right of every child to an decent education. These cuts will close the doors of hope to our nation's most vulnerable young people."

Other participants in the press conference were LauraLee Summer, a Harvard undergraduate student who was formerly homeless; and, Maria Foscarinis, executive director and founder of the National Law Center on Homelessness and Poverty.

Also participating in the press conference were Rep. Louise Slaughter (D-NY) and Rep. Bruce Vento (D-MN), two Members of Congress who have lead the fight for federal programs to help end homelessness.

The National Coalition for the Homeless is a Washington-based grassroots advocacy group seeking an end to homelessness. NCH has affilates in every state.

1612 K Street, NW, #1004, Washington, DC 20006 • 202-775-1322 • Fax 202-775-1316

A well-written news release like this one would be more effective with a headline. Credit: National Coalition for the Homeless

Different Kinds of Releases

Some public relations experts use numerous kinds of releases—
for events, features, background information, a calendar item.
One basic release, however, will work fine. What's important is
what's written on the release and who receives it at a news organization. However, you may wish to modify your news release
slightly for a news advisory or a calendar item.

As Paul Day from KCNC-TV in Denver put it, "If we haven't
grabbed our viewers in thirty seconds, we haven't done our job."
If your release doesn't grab a reader in ten seconds, you haven't
done yours.

A release will seldom, if ever, convince a reporter to write a feature, which is a magazine-like article that is not based on breaking news. To convince a reporter to write a feature, you'll need to
call feature writers, preferably ones you know, and "chat them
up" on the phone. Or pitch a feature idea to reporters who attend
your event or press conference or who call you for a comment on
a breaking story. (See Chapter 18, "Pitch a Feature Story.")

A News Advisory

News advisories have two purposes. First, use them to alert journalists to an event that you know is not on the top of their agendas but that might interest them. It's akin to an FYI, written in a
simple form without details. The second purpose of a news advisory: If you have information that you want to keep secret until a
news conference, send out a news advisory stating where and
when the news conference will be and what the topic is. (You'll
have a difficult time attracting the media to a news conference
unless you state what you plan to release or unless your organization's track record has made it clear that when you hold a news
conference, it's because you have newsworthy information to dis-
seminate.)

A news advisory is written just like a regular news release with the appropriate date, phone numbers, and contact people. Following is a sample.

Planned Parenthood®
of the Rocky Mountains

The mission of Planned Parenthood of the Rocky Mountains is to improve the quality of life by enabling all people voluntarily to exercise individual choice in their own fertility and reproductive health.

MEDIA ADVISORY   CONTACT:
June 6, 1997   Kate Reinisch: 321-PLAN (7526)

Planned Parenthood Honors Graduates of Their Teen Pregnancy Prevention Programs
Community Leaders and Sports Stars Celebrate
High-Risk Teens Who Beat The Odds

What: Reception and Graduation Ceremony for *Dollar-A-Day* and *Male Achievement Network* Graduates

When: Tuesday, June 10, 1997
Event: 5:30 to 7:00 PM
Media Availability with Teens: 5:00 to 5:30 PM

Where: The Governor's Mansion, 400 E. Eighth Ave., Denver

Speakers: (Letter of support from Jane Fonda and Ted Turner will be read)
Dani Newsum, KHOW Radio
Lark Birdsong and Missy Masley, Colorado Xplosion
Mark Knudsen, Colorado Rockies
Graduates of PPRM's Teen Pregnancy Prevention Programs

Agenda: 5:00 PM   Media availability
                 5:30 PM   Event begins
                 6:00 PM   Ceremony begins
                 6:30 PM   Ceremony ends
                 7:00 PM   Event ends

Dollar A Day: An innovative teen pregnancy program which utilizes mentoring, professional counselors, education, peer support and a token monetary incentive to empower at-risk young women to delay pregnancy. PPRM has 7 *Dollar A Day* groups with a 94% success rate.

Male Achievement Network (MAN): The intent of *MAN* is to encourage young men to make responsible life choices regarding their sexuality and involvement in teen pregnancy. *MAN* groups meet at 7 high schools and provide participants with role models, support, information and education.

###

950 Broadway, Denver, Colorado 80203-2779 • 303-321-PLAN • FAX 303-861-0268 • Clinic Appointment 1-800-230-PLAN • Facts of Life Line (303) 832-5995

A news advisory contains even fewer details than a news release. Credit: Planned Parenthood of the Rocky Mountains

A Calendar Item

If you've got an event you'd like included in the community calendars of newspapers or other media, use the style of a news release to distribute the information. Make sure the essential information is clearly printed on the release. Label it "Calendar Item" and make sure you send it to the appropriate people at news outlets. Following is a sample. (See Chapter 27, "Use Community Calendars and Public Service Announcements.")

FOR IMMEDIATE RELEASE   March 26, 1998
Contact: Jason Salzman
303-832-7558

CALENDAR ITEM
NEW BOOK HELPS CITIZENS IMPROVE THEIR MEDIA SKILLS

Author to Discuss New Book at Tattered Cover Bookstore Downtown

Wednesday, April 22, from Noon to 1 P.M.

Lecture to Feature Slides of Newsworthy Visual Imagery and Symbols

WHAT: Jason Salzman will sign his new book, *Making the News: A Guide for Nonprofits and Activists,* now available at bookstores.

Making the News contains simple, concise information on how to write news releases; contact reporters; create newsworthy visual imagery; book a guest on talk radio; lobby editorial writers, columnists, and photographers; and much more.

The book is based on interviews with professional journalists and activists.

WHERE: Tattered Cover Bookstore in LoDo, 1628 16th Street (16th and Wynkoop)

WHEN: Wednesday, April 22, noon to 1 P.M.
WHY: It's easy to complain about the news and accuse journal-
        ists of doing a poor job, but citizens can be as much to
        blame as reporters for bad journalism, according to *Mak-
        ing the News.*

Activists need to improve their media skills by offering journalists
more quality information—in the right packaging at the right time.

—30—

Video for TV

If you're releasing a story and you've got "background footage"
to go with it, state on your news release that video is available.
Such videotape, called "B-roll," can give your story the video appeal it needs to make television news. Home video is widely used
in newscasts, especially on local TV news. If you've got a dramatic home video, you can turn it into a story all by itself.

"It always helps to advance a story if there is home video that
goes along with it," says Tom Donahue, Miami bureau chief for
CBS News. "Quite often, we'll buy it."

Embargoes

If you "embargo" a news release, you are—in theory—prohibit-
ing journalists from using your information until some future
date. For example, if you are distributing a document to reporters
on May 3 and do not want any coverage until May 7, you would
type "Embargo until 9 A.M. May 7" on the top of the release.
You'd expect your story, if it were newsworthy, to appear in
evening papers and on television and radio on May 7 and in
morning papers on May 8. News services such as AP would distribute it on May 7.

You should avoid placing an embargo on a news release.
Here's why:

- News media commonly break embargoes or find a way to get around them.
- Advance coverage of an event usually leads to more coverage, not less.
- Generally, you should take coverage when you can get it. Tomorrow the sky may fall or a plane may crash, and you could get no coverage at all.
- Reporters may not take kindly to an embargo. "Most of the time, it's arrogant for a special interest group to embargo," says Mark Obmascik, a columnist at the *Denver Post*.

One type of release, however, may merit an embargo. If you're releasing a lengthy report, you should consider giving reporters a couple of extra days to study it and perhaps get some reactions to it.

If you do embargo a release, do not distribute it widely. It should be sent only to reporters you know. Unless you have an ongoing relationship with a reporter, you're taking a substantial risk by giving him or her your breaking-news story before the release date.

I've repeatedly seen reporters break embargoes. Once, I explicitly told a well-known columnist at *USA Today* not to publish information about a report before the release date printed clearly on our news release. I opened up *USA Today* the next morning—one day before our release date—and there was a short piece about our report buried deep in the paper.

Another time, I helped line up four reporters, including one from the *New York Times*, who were interested in writing a story about a report I was releasing. My organization sent the report with an embargo request to each of them, including a reporter from the Associated Press, in advance. The AP reporter received our report and broke the embargo, publishing it a day before the release date. This resulted in the *Times* deciding not to cover our story. Fortunately, however, the AP put our story on the national wire and it was distributed to media outlets across the country.

10

Distribute a News Release

ONCE YOU'VE GOT A MEDIA LIST, getting your news release out should be easy. In fact, with a computer program and a modem, you can fax or e-mail a release to an entire list of reporters with the push of a button.

No matter how you deliver your news release, you should make follow-up calls to be sure journalists received it. (See Chapter 12, "Call a Reporter After You've Sent a News Release.")

How Should You Deliver Your News Release?

By Fax

Most reporters prefer to receive news releases by fax even though they are inundated with them. At national and local outlets alike, journalists might receive twenty-five faxes per day in addition to regular mail, e-mail, and phone calls.

"It's still best to send faxes," says David Briscoe, the Associated Press's chief correspondent for international services in Washington, D.C. "But eventually it will be e-mail."

By Mail

Regular mail also works, but reporters receive even more "snail mail" than faxes. If you mail your release, experiment with addressing the envelopes by hand—or send a postcard that need not be opened. As one newspaper editor told me, "If it's hand-addressed, you never know what it's going to be. If it is type-written or computer generated, it can wait."

"A blind mailing from an unknown organization is least likely to get attention," says Tom Lippman, a diplomatic correspondent at the *Washington Post*. "It gets the attention of the circular file."

By E-mail

E-mail is an electronic system for sending information from one computer to another via the Internet. Sending a news release by e-mail to journalists is unreliable because not all of them use it, especially at local outlets—at least not yet. Probably about half the computers journalists use at local outlets across the country are *not* hooked up to the Internet. And even when e-mail is available, many reporters—like other professionals—don't bother with it. "I'm not an e-mail person," says Tom Lippman at the *Washington Post*. "I go days without checking my e-mail. It's a technology that's been grafted on to me in middle age."

E-mail can, however, be a very effective way to communicate with reporters who use it. "E-mail's best," says Keith Rogers, a reporter for the *Las Vegas Review-Journal*. "If I'm not interested, I can hit the clear button and it's gone. . . . I've covered entire stories through e-mail—sending questions and getting answers back. It's easier to e-mail than pick up the phone and call."

To compile an e-mail list, make a point to ask journalists for their e-mail addresses. You can also access an e-mail directory on the Web (www.four11.com) that lists e-mail addresses of people around the world. The directory is not comprehensive, but it's worth a try. You can also try to locate a business or individual who maintains a list. For now, the use of e-mail distribution services is most applicable to organizations working at the national level on specialized subjects.

Another option is to try to locate a Web site where news releases are posted. For example, EurekAlert!, which has the backing of professional scientific societies, posts news releases for top science writers on its Web site (www.eurekalert.org/).

Even if all journalists are *not* using e-mail regularly, most conduct research on the Web, which can be accessed in most newsrooms. If possible, your organization should maintain a Web site containing information about you and your cause.

By Hand

Hand delivering your release to news outlets is unnecessary. In fact, you can't even get through the front office of some news organizations without a scheduled appointment. However, if a reporter who expressed an interest in your event did not show up, you should hand deliver to him or her a release and other information that you distributed at your event.

By Satellite

Some large corporations spend big money sending a "video news release" (VNR) to local TV stations via satellite. However, VNRs do not appear to be used enough by local stations to justify the price. (For a discussion of VNRs, see the *Publicity Handbook*, listed in Chapter 38, "Media How-To Books.")

When Should a Release Be Distributed?

A news release should arrive at an outlet no earlier than a week before an event and no later than the day before. If you send it more than a week in advance, it will likely get lost—although some outlets claim that they want to receive releases two to three weeks in advance. Place your follow-up call the day before your event. Call again the morning of your event. If you're working on a feature story, you should begin your outreach to feature writers many weeks in advance. (See Chapter 18, "Pitch a Feature Story.")

How Many Reporters at a Single Outlet Should Receive the Release?

Generally, you should not contact two journalists at a single news outlet. However, if a news reporter at a large newspaper tells you that your event isn't newsworthy and he or she will *not* cover it, you should think of a way to convince a columnist or a reporter from, say, the business section to cover it. You should not pitch a story to two reporters in the same department, for example, two business reporters. (For information on whom you should contact at different news outlets, see Chapter 8, "Compile a Media List.")

"The biggest mistake groups make with the Associated Press is sending their news releases to too many people in the office," says David Briscoe at the Associated Press, echoing sentiments by other journalists. "All of us end up throwing them away."

Send Your Release to Daybooks

Each day at 5 or 6 A.M., the Associated Press sends its sub-scribers—which probably include all major news outlets in your area—a "daybook" listing news events scheduled to take place in the region on that day. Someone at most major news outlets re-views the daybook each morning.

The daybook includes all kinds of news events. "We'll put al-most anything on there, with the exception of entertainment events and anything of a money-making nature," says Bill Schiff-mann, a news editor for AP's San Francisco bureau. A daybook for most cities typically contains five to ten items and may be up-dated to include breaking events during the day.

To have your event considered for the daybook, your news release should arrive at the AP by the morning of the day *before* your event. Address it to the "daybook editor." If appropriate, type "photo available" on the release.

In some cities, different news services publish competing daybooks, for example, AP and Reuters in Washington, D.C. Make sure your event is listed in all of them. (For more information on the Associated Press and other news services, see Chapter 8, "Compile a Media List," and Chapter 30, "Promote a Story to Journalists at National News Outlets.")

11

Become a
Master Interviewee

Y**OU SHOULD PREPARE THOROUGHLY** for any meeting with a reporter—whether it takes place at an event you organize or in your office in response to a reporter's request for an interview. The more time you have to prepare, the greater the chances the interview will go smoothly.

Never consider yourself so experienced at dealing with journalists that you needn't prepare for interviews. The most visible spokespeople—including the president of the United States—spend considerable time polishing their interview skills and practicing their lines. Your advance preparation for interviews should consist of developing your message, creating sound bites, anticipating questions, and practicing your delivery of answers and sound bites.

Develop Your Message

In most interviews with reporters, you should focus on one message. Depending on the length of the interview, however, you should prepare additional supporting points. For example, if your simple message is that local TV news reports too much crime, you could be prepared with (1) murder is usually the lead story on local TV news; (2) crime rates are down but crime coverage is increasing on local TV news; and (3) local TV news stations dedicate more time to crime coverage than any other topic.

If you anticipate a long one-on-one interview or a lengthy session on talk radio, you'll want to stick to your message and weave in your supporting points during your conversation, repeating them for emphasis. Even in the longest interviews, you will rarely be able to cover more than three to six points to support your message. If you're staging a stunt or an image-based event, however, it's likely that you'll have time to make only one point to support your message. (See "Tips for TV Interviews" later in the chapter.)

Deliver your message and supporting points in a way that is conducive to the space requirements and style of the outlet. For example, if you are being interviewed for a news radio program, give the journalist a sound bite that's appropriate for radio news. This will maximize the chances that your central message—not some tangential point—will be conveyed to the public.

Create Sound Bites

A sound bite is the type of speech commonly found on television and radio broadcasts. (Print reporters quote sound bites, too, but the ones they use are often less dramatic than the ones for TV and radio.) A sound bite is defined by how long it takes to deliver (five to twelve seconds) and by the style of language it contains. Use action verbs in sound bites.

You will want to develop sound bites not only for your central message but also for any additional points that support your message. Often, the most quotable sound bites are connected to the actual imagery of your event. For example, a nuclear reactor in Texas had had a long history of deficiencies and was widely regarded as a "lemon." To protest the restart of this plant, activists dressed as lemons and used this sound bite: "Restarting this reactor would sour the economy of Texas."

Similarly, activists in New Mexico donned Pinocchio noses to illustrate their point that the governor of New Mexico was stretching the truth about the safety of a waste dump. The sound bite they chose: "The truth about the governor's position is as plain as the nose on my face."

Sound bites related to the earlier message that local TV news reports too much crime include "There's a lot more happening in Dallas than murders, but you wouldn't know it from watching local TV news"; "If it bleeds, it leads"; and "A steady diet of crime on TV is unbalanced and unhealthy."

If you're in a rush and need to create a good sound bite, start it with the phrase "I'm here today to . . ." If you want to highlight your organization, start the same phrase with your organization's name. Following are more sample sound bites.

"People Against Police Violence is here today to stop the police brutality before it stops us."

"My yard is contaminated. Where are my kids going to play?"

"Recycle America should change its name to 'Dump on China,' because it isn't recycling plastic; it's dumping it on China."

"If the Norwegian government is unwilling to stop the whale hunt, we'll make them stop."

"This law has nothing to do with medicine and everything to do with politics."

Anticipate Interview Questions

You should try to predict the questions you'll be asked in an interview. What are the typical arguments against your position? What problems has your organization faced? Look over recent articles about your issue and note the types of questions asked. You also need to have answers ready about your funding and history. Following are some typical questions asked by interviewers.

Why are you out here today?
Why are you releasing this report?
What's the point of this protest?
Do you really think this will have an impact?
Isn't this just a publicity stunt?
What's next?
Who's funding your organization?
How long have you been in existence?
Are you just an idealist?

In most interviews, you'll face questions you did not think of in advance. Sometimes you can make a prepared answer fit a surprise question, but if it doesn't fit, you shouldn't force it. Especially when you're facing a print journalist, you should answer questions directly.

Practice Your Answers and Sound Bites

You won't regret practicing your answers and sound bites. Assign someone to ask you the questions you think a journalist might ask. Remember that journalists are busy and have probably had less time to prepare for the interview than you. They frequently fall back on stock questions, which often leave you lots of room to say what you want.

Avoid Talking to a Journalist "Off the Record"

Sometimes, a "source"—like you—will speak to a journalist only under specific conditions. For example, a source might offer information to a reporter but not want his or her name associated with it. (Sometimes this is called "off the record.") Or a source might not want his or her quote—or any information relayed during a conversation—used at all. (Sometimes this is called "background.") The trouble is, journalists interpret terms like "off the record" differently. For example, if you are the spokesperson for a human rights organization and you are speaking "off the record" or "not for attribution," does that mean your anonymous quote cannot be attributed to an "unnamed human rights group" or to the "human rights community" or to an "activist"?

Speak to journalists "on the record." There is usually no need for a spokesperson for a nonprofit organization to operate any other way. This means everything you say can be attributed to you, even something as casual as "Let me take off my rumpled jacket for this photo." Steve Trombulak of Middlebury College once told a reporter his personal opinion of logging-company executives. Only later did he realize his expletives might end up in print. They did.

Furthermore, your willingness to speak on the record attracts journalists: "[Nonprofit groups] are willing to say on the record what others aren't willing to say," says Tom Lippman, a diplomatic reporter for the *Washington Post*.

If you must place conditions on your conversation with journalists—and you have clear strategic reasons for doing so—don't use vague terms such as "off the record." Instead, explain to each journalist the specific conditions under which your information can be used. If you decide that only part of a long conversation should *not* be on the record, make sure you make it very clear when you are talking on the record and when you are not.

Tips for TV Interviews

- Determine the format. Will your interview be taped and edited later, like many local TV news interviews? Will it be live, like *Larry King Live*? Or will it be live on tape, like many public affairs programs and some TV talk shows?

TV interviews can be conducted either on location or in a TV studio with or without a reporter present. Live interviews can be more stressful, but look at them as an opportunity to send an unedited message to your audience.

- If you're staging an event, your TV interviews will probably be conducted at the site of your event with or without a reporter. If a reporter accompanies the camera operator to your event, it's more likely your event will appear on the news. (Sometimes the camera operator and the reporter are the same person.)

- I advise people, overall, to dress conservatively for television—to avoid alienating the audience with their clothes. (There was a day when solid colors were recommended because plaids looked busy or even melted together. Today, you should worry less about the restrictions of technology and more about what colors look good on you.)

- Make your own decision about what jewelry looks good on you. Think about whether your jewelry (e.g., a nose ring) will make people disregard what you say. Flashy earrings will be even more flashy if the TV camera zooms in on your face.

- Hats with a brim may cast a shadow across your face. Avoid them.

- You don't need makeup for television unless you feel you need it in the real, non-TV world. And you probably won't be offered any makeup prior to a TV interview. That said, if it's offered to you at a studio, you might as well accept it. (It's the same logic as "a little tan never hurts your appearance.") But if you look in the mirror and see that your makeup job looks bad (e.g., clownlike), for goodness' sake get it off before you go on the air!

- Perspiration can be a problem, especially for bald people. If it's a big problem for you, you should consider applying powder prior to your interview and possibly during commercials. You can bring your own powder to your interview site.

- Bring a copy of your report or book for a close-up shot.
- Warm up your voice by talking for a few minutes before your interview.
- Breathe deeply before the interview.
- Speak slowly in five- to twelve-second sentences.
- Use action verbs in the present tense. Be forceful.
- Relax your shoulders and keep your body still.
- Don't lean forward, particularly if you're being interviewed indoors under bright lights. (The lights will cast shadows across your face if you move forward, making you look villain-like.)
- Make hand gestures or hold a prop.
- If you are standing at a podium, don't lean forward. The camera operators adjust the microphones to pick up your voice while you are standing up straight.
- Look at the reporter or the camera operator. Do not look into cameras unless you are conversing from the field with the anchor back at the studio. (Ask the camera operator where to look if you are unsure.)
- Give brief answers to questions. The more tape they've got, the less control *you've* got over what gets on the air.
- Time zooms by when you're on TV. Get your highest-priority points out as soon as possible.
- If you're being taped and you think you've screwed up a sound bite, stop and repeat it. If you stutter or mispronounce a word, apologize and start again.
- If you're live on camera and the reporter is harassing you or a crowd around you is causing confusion, you can look into the camera and say something directly to the audience. This can be effective, but it should be used rarely because it can look canned and annoy the reporter at the site. (Once a police officer was being interviewed about whether a mur-

derer would be caught. He looked directly into the live TV cameras and told the murderer out there that he would, indeed, be caught. This attempt at drama looked silly.)

- Interpret questions very broadly or, if necessary, ignore them completely and say what you want. This especially applies to TV interviews, in which many reporters will only take a sound bite and be on their way.
- Raise and lower your voice (and possibly your eyebrows) to make a point.
- Don't read a prepared statement.
- Deliver a sound bite in the form of a question. This is an excellent way to frame an issue and prompt a response from your opponents (e.g., "Can they prove that the factory is safe?").
- Give examples that are as personal as possible. TV reporters are looking for emotion. Refer to concrete images.
- If necessary, ask to add a final comment to a taped interview.
- Expect, at the end of some taped interviews, a camera operator to shoot "cutaway" shots of you and the reporter talking. Often the back of your head will be photographed—or possibly the reporter asking questions. This footage can be inserted in the final story for editing purposes.
- Some TV stations have "beat" reporters who cover issue areas. You should recognize these reporters and be prepared for more detailed questions from them than you get from your average TV reporter.
- If you've got video footage that's relevant to the interview topic, offer it to the producer or reporter. Stations will sometimes use this "B-roll" footage for background shots.

Tips for Radio Interviews

From an activist's perspective, radio news interviews are much like those for television news, except, of course, they require good audio instead of video. Thus many of the tips for television interviews apply to radio with the following caveats:

- Warm up your voice prior to the interview by singing or yelling at your dog. (See Chapter 25, "Tune Your Cause to Talk Radio," for more tips on what to do before you go on the air.)
- Don't worry about speaking slowly on the radio as long as you speak clearly.
- Try to provide other sounds—besides voice—for radio (e.g., chants, cheers, clapping, relevant music).
- A story on public radio may include a twenty- to thirty-second quotation. But you will seldom hear a sound bite of more than ten or fifteen seconds on commercial radio.
- The majority of radio interviews, like print interviews, are conducted by phone. Make sure your phone is in a quiet place, and—if you're live on the air—do not listen to the radio while you're being interviewed. There is a delay and it will confuse you. The delay can also cause the screeching sound known as "feedback."
- Radio audiences are largest during rush hour. Try to get on the radio at this time.

Tips for Print Media Interviews

Newspaper reporters, who often cover "beats" (issue areas), are more likely to engage in a detailed discussion of your issue than most broadcast journalists. Generally, there is more space in a newspaper to explain the subtleties of an issue. As a result, print journalists will likely ask for more quantifiable information and be less satisfied with broad rhetorical statements from you.

Nonetheless, it makes sense to practice delivering sound bites to print reporters. "Reporters have their ears open for a phrase that's going to ring," says *Rocky Mountain News* reporter Bill Scanlon. "There is nothing wrong with practicing."

- Avoid wild rhetoric that's more suited for TV.
- Don't ignore questions. Newspaper reporters usually want more precise answers to their questions than do TV interviewers.
- Ask a reporter to read back a quote of yours only if absolutely necessary. Reserve this for extremely critical quotes.
- Print reporters are more likely to appreciate irony.
- Most print journalists will interview by phone, but you should dress conservatively for personal interviews.
- Sometimes a print journalist simply wants a response to some event over the phone. This type of story is called a "reaction piece." You can often predict when you will get such calls and have a statement ready to read, allowing you to deliver a precise quote. (See Chapter 17, "Suggest Ideas for News Stories to Journalists.")

Tips for Becoming a Master Interviewee

No matter what type of interview you are anticipating, certain fundamentals apply:

- An interview is never over even if the tape stops rolling. Everything you say to a journalist should be considered on the record.
- Be courteous to all media people, including camera operators and support staff.
- Never assume journalists are on your side even though they will often act as if they are.
- You should feel free to make a statement, then answer the question (e.g., "I'll answer that, but first, by way of background, I want to say . . .").
- Eliminate insider jargon and acronyms specific to your area of expertise from your speech.
- Never say "no comment." If you cannot talk about a subject, explain why.

- Keep your answers short, drawing on your message and supporting points that you practiced for the interview.
- Don't address the reporter by name constantly. It sounds stilted.
- You can use either a reporter's first or last name depending on your style.
- Journalists like anecdotes.
- Stick to the facts. Remember, you don't have to answer hypothetical questions. If a question is speculative, say so and add that you'll answer it if the hypothetical situation becomes reality.
- There is not one type of "media personality." Be yourself.
- Even the most experienced spokespeople are nervous during interviews. Get used to the feeling and realize that your nervous energy can help you be more lucid.
- Tell a reporter what you think is the most important angle for him or her to write about.
- Humor is great if it's not cutesy. (Many journalists are, understandably, quite cynical and therefore relate to cynical humor.)
- Suggest questions that reporters should ask of your opponents. It may also be appropriate to suggest questions journalists should ask *you*.
- If you need more time to think, ask the reporter to repeat the question or ask a clarifying question—or simply pause and think before answering.
- If you don't know the answer to a question, say so. Track down the answer later and call the reporter.
- Tell a reporter you have more to add if he or she overlooks something you think is important.
- Dress as you want to appear. But remember your goal and audience. It's a shame when casual or ragged clothes distract your audience from what you are saying. Also think about the stereotypical image of someone who's fighting

for your cause. Do you want to go with that or perhaps dress to appeal to somebody besides the "choir"?

- Get to know the reporters in your community so that you can present information in language that meshes with their particular style, making it more likely that you'll be quoted. Respect the professional relationship you have with reporters.

How to Conduct Yourself After an Interview

You should be courteous, but not gushing, to all media personnel. They will thank you, and you should return the thank-you and suggest they call if they need further information. One time a talk-radio host beat me up for a full hour—cut me off, attributed statements to me that I did not make, even claimed I lived in a city that I did not live in, and was generally rude. I thanked him at the end, saying that some hosts wouldn't ask guests with different views to be on their shows. He told me to announce the name and phone number of my organization on the air. Then he asked me to repeat it.

Make sure to take time to watch tapes of the shows you're on and read clips with your quotes. You'll find ways to improve. (Plus, it's fun.)

12

Call a Reporter After You've Sent a News Release

You could have the country's best event, the planet's best news release, the universe's most up-to-date media list, and be blessed in heaven—and all of it may not matter unless you make follow-up calls to make sure journalists know about your event.

Faxing, mailing, or e-mailing a release to a reporter does not guarantee that he or she will see it. Mail gets lost, chewed, ignored, or buried. At some outlets, the faxes pile up in oblivion unless a journalist makes a special effort to retrieve one. "I get stacks of faxes," says Craig Maclaine, a reporter for Radio Canada International, the external news service of the Canadian Broadcasting Corporation. "I get through the first ten and the rest disappear."

"It's a lot easier to ignore a piece of paper than a phone call," says *Albuquerque Journal* reporter John Fleck. "You get faxed to death," says Michael Hirsh, a Washington, D.C., correspondent for *Newsweek*. "Regular mail is even worse. I throw out half without opening it. Absolutely the best way is to call."

Some communications directors at nonprofit organizations delegate follow-up calls to new volunteers or entry-level staff. This is a mistake because chances are the follow-up call will play a large role in determining whether a reporter covers your event. Also, phone calls offer you a chance to interact with journalists and develop credibility.

"A follow-up call can make the difference in getting on the air," says Leonard Nelson, producer of KNBR radio's morning show in San Francisco. "If you're persistent, you stand a better chance." Few journalists have layers of secretaries. You can get through. Keep trying.

Never assume you don't need to call. Once, a rally I organized was covered in advance by a major metropolitan daily newspaper. Because the paper had already informed its readers the rally was happening, I figured that I didn't need to call to remind editors to send a reporter to the event. No reporter from the paper showed. The rally had slipped through the cracks. I should have called.

Tips for an Effective Follow-up Call

- Call the Associated Press "daybook editor" to make sure your event is listed in the daybook (For information on the AP daybook, see Chapter 10, "Distribute a News Release.") Make this call first.
- Call journalists the morning of *the day before* your event even if you've made contact weeks before. (For information on which journalists to call, see Chapter 8, "Compile a Media List.")
- Call editors between 11 A.M. and 1 P.M. because they usually have morning meetings. Call reporters early in the day. "The worst time ever to call is when we're on deadline," says Keith Rogers, a reporter for the *Las Vegas Review-Journal*. "I've got a story that's got to get done, and the clock is ticking."
- Call television stations again the morning of your event.
- Don't trust voice mail. Reach a person—not a machine. (As a last resort, you can call at night and talk to the night editor.)
- Identify yourself and ask if the release has been received.

- If it has not arrived, say you'll fax a copy. Ask if the journalist has a minute to hear about the event on the phone. If so, make a thirty-second pitch about the event, which you should practice in advance (see the examples further on). "I don't have time to sit on the phone for twenty minutes and find out there's no story there," says Craig Maclaine at Radio Canada International.
- Call again to make sure your news release was received after you faxed it a second time.
- If the journalist has received your release, ask if he or she has any questions. (Ask in a way that explains your event: "Do you have any questions about our 10 A.M. news conference tomorrow at the jail to announce our new initiative on violence prevention?")
- If you are making lots of long distance follow-up calls—and your budget is tight—let the phone ring twice and hang up before the answering machine picks up. Most journalists answer the phone after the first ring if they're taking calls. Keep calling back until you get a person.
- Don't give up. Be persistent.

Four Sample Follow-up Calls

By the time you're making follow-up calls, you should already have identified a specific journalist to pitch your story to. (See Chapter 8, "Compile a Media List," for tips on whom to contact.) And you should have addressed your release directly to him or her. (Never send a fax to, say, the *Baltimore Sun* without a name attached to it.) If you have not selected a specific journalist, your call will probably be routed to a student intern or possibly an editor. Your event may still be covered, but you're better off when you know whom you want to reach.

You don't need to waste time saying your name unless you're known to the journalist. Say, "I'm calling from . . ." rather than "I'm Jane Button from . . ."

Sample Follow-up Call for a
TV Assignment Editor or TV Reporter

You: Hello, I'm calling from People for a Liveable Downtown to make sure you received our news release about our plans to release giant balloons to show how ugly the new skyscraper will look downtown. Five neighborhood groups are opposing construction of the building.

Assignment Editor: Let me check. . . . I don't see it.

You: We're releasing the balloons tomorrow to dramatize how massive the new skyscraper will be. I'll fax the release again right now.

Assignment Editor: Thank you.

At least half the time, reporters will not be able to locate your faxed news release when you call. You should fax it again and call again to make sure it was received the second time.

Another Sample Follow-up Call for a
TV Assignment Editor or TV Reporter

You: Hello, I'm calling from People for a Liveable Downtown to make sure you received our press release about our balloon protest tomorrow at 10 A.M. in front of the train station.

Assignment Editor: Hold on. . . . Yes, now I've got it.

You: We believe the proposed skyscraper would ruin the character of the city for the loft-dwelling residents, and we don't think people understand just how big the skyscraper will be. That's why we're going to tie the giant balloons to a string and let them rise to the height of the proposed building.

Assignment Editor: When will this take place?

You: Tomorrow, Wednesday, at 10 A.M. in front of the train station downtown. A few neighborhood leaders will speak; then we'll release the giant, colorful balloons.

Assignment Editor: We'll probably send someone down there.
You: Thank you.

When you are pitching a story to a television journalist, remember that the substance of the story is of equal or lesser value than the video possibilities. Always emphasize the visual components of your story. If you don't have any, you'd better think of some if you want TV coverage.

Sample Follow-up Call for a Newspaper Editor or Reporter

You: Hello, I'm calling from Rocky Mountain Media Watch to make sure you received our press release about our report documenting that crime coverage on local TV news is up while national crime rates are dropping.
Reporter: Do you have something in writing?
You: Yes, I just sent you a fax describing our report covering local TV news in 100 cities, including your city.
Reporter: I'll look for it. When did you send it?
You: I just faxed it.
Reporter: Hold on a minute. . . . Yes, I've got it here.
You: You'll notice that the number of murder stories on local TV news in your city doubled over the past year, but the murder rate is down in your area.
Reporter: What group are you with?
You: Rocky Mountain Media Watch has conducted annual studies of local TV news since 1994. Our reports have received national coverage in the past, and your predecessor covered our report last year.
Reporter: I'm in the middle of something else right now. Where are you going to be in an hour?
You: You can reach me at the phone number on the press release all day.

Reporter: Thank you.
You: Would you like me to fax over the five-page executive summary?
Reporter: Yes. Do that.
You: Thank you. I'm looking forward to speaking with you later.

Newspaper reporters are usually interested in stories with new information from credible sources. In this case, the reporter seems to be interested in the story. Otherwise, he would not have asked where to reach you or requested the executive summary. In the previous example, it would make sense for you to call again in a couple of hours even if you do not receive a call first. You might say that you wanted to make sure that he received your second fax.

Another Sample Follow-up Call for a Newspaper Reporter or Editor

You: Hello, I'm calling from Rocky Mountain Media Watch to make sure you received our press release about our report documenting that crime coverage on local TV news is up while national crime rates are dropping.
Reporter: Yes, I just received your fax.
You: You'll note that your city had more stories about robberies on local TV news than any other city. Yet robberies are down in your area. Do you have any questions about our report?
Reporter: No.
You: Is this a story you or someone else there might be interested in?
Reporter: We just ran a two-part series on the local anchors that touched on this.
You: Yes, I saw that. It was an interesting piece—a fair and balanced treatment of the subject, I thought. But our report

focuses more on the content of the news rather than on the personalities of the anchors. Maybe there's something different in our report.

Reporter: I don't think so. We asked them about the crime coverage, and they justified it.

You: Well, thank you for your time.

Reporter: Let me know when your next report comes out.

You: I sure will.

You have to be able to lose gracefully. It hurts in the short term, but it pays later because you leave the impression with the reporter that you are a reasonable professional whom she can call for information. You should gently try to convince a reporter to cover your story, but you should not argue. "Not every news release groups fax us will get in the paper," says Jack Broom, a reporter at the *Seattle Times*. "They shouldn't give up."

For stories with good visual imagery, also make a follow-up call to the photo department. At larger papers, ask for the photo assignment editor or the photo editor. At television stations, there is no need to make a separate call to camera operators. (See Chapter 23, "Influence Newspaper Photographers.")

Don't think journalists are doing you a favor by covering your event. Remember that journalists rely on sources like you to feed them story ideas and information. They need you as much as you need them. "It's my job to listen to people, and I try to do that," says Tom Lippman, a diplomatic correspondent at the *Washington Post*.

13

Hold a
News Conference

WHEN MANY CONCERNED CITIZENS and activists think of publicity, what pops into their minds is "news conference." In reality, a news conference is usually the wrong way to attract the media. It's a much better idea to call reporters and fax them information or, if you're staging an event, to have a spokesperson available to give individual interviews as requested. (See Chapter 4, "Create Newsworthy Visual Imagery, Symbols, and Stunts.")

"Simply covering a news conference doesn't happen very often," says Cathy McFeaters, news director at KVUE-TV, Austin's ABC affiliate. But news conferences may be the right approach if you expect significant coverage or if you are having an event and will not have time for personal interviews there.

If a news conference is called for, the appropriate timing and location would be the same as for other types of media events. (See Chapter 5, "Choose a Time to Maximize Coverage," and Chapter 6, "Find an Effective Location.") Whenever possible, hold press conferences outside with backup arrangements for bad weather. You don't have to worry about providing electricity for lights and cameras.

Tips for Staging a News Conference

- Practice the news conference in advance, including questions.

- Place your group's logo in front of the podium.
- Make sure your amplification system is adequate.
- Assign someone to greet reporters and to ask them to write their names on a "sign-in" sheet.
- Plan for a maximum of four speakers. There's usually no need for any speaker to drone on longer than five minutes. Put your most important speakers on first.
- Create props for your speakers to hold, especially if they are the only visual element of your event. Speakers might stand beside and gesture toward large (two-foot by three-foot) charts or diagrams, which can be made at copy stores.
- Speakers should dress in formal clothes unless they are in costumes or their clothes are somehow related to the message they are trying to send. (Many activists eschew dressing up, as if it were a litmus test of their sincerity. But why go to all the effort of trying to reach mainstream media and then distract or, worse, alienate your audience by wearing unusual clothes?)
- Be aware that photographers frequently arrive at press conferences early to get a candid photo of participants doing something besides standing in front of a podium. Make sure your candid shot is the one you want by preparing for photographers who come early.
- TV crews often shoot the news conference room. These shots look better if the majority of the seats are filled. Have supporters on hand to fill empty seats.
- If only a few reporters arrive on time, delay five minutes or longer to see if more show up. But if you've got a sizable group assembled—particularly TV cameras—get started on time. You can't predict when the next carjacking will send the TV cameras running off.
- A moderator should cut off speakers who run on too long.
- Allow ten minutes for questions.

- A news conference should seldom last longer than a half-hour. Journalists who want more information can ask questions after the event.
- Do not restrict your press conference to journalists, but be prepared for disruptions (see further on).

Assemble a Press Packet

Easy-to-read information should be distributed to journalists at your event. If you have more than three pieces of paper, put them in a folder with your organization's logo on it. This is called a press packet.

It's always tempting to make the mistake of giving a journalist too much written information. You will impress a journalist much more by demonstrating that you recognize his or her real needs. Journalists obtain most of their information from conversations, not from written sources. Don't feed the recycling bins in the newsroom. Keep your press packets simple and slim. Following is a list of materials for a press packet.

- Your news release
- Brief biographies of speakers at your event
- Two recent articles about your cause
- One feature article, a summary of a report, or any piece of more in-depth information

Disruptions at a Press Conference

Once I was in the middle of speaking at a news conference at the unveiling of a series of twelve billboards at the gates of the Rocky Flats nuclear-bomb plant near Denver. I must have been saying something right because suddenly a man from the audience started denouncing Greenpeace and me. He shouted, and the TV cameras started to swing toward him. We had about 100 people at the news conference, far outnumbering the protester.

Inspired by Allen Ginsberg's Buddhist chants at 1960s demonstrations, I initiated a chant among the audience. "Close Rocky Flats," we chanted, completely drowning out the single protester's cries and showing for the television cameras how small a minority he represented. He eventually quieted and we continued with our speeches.

This response to a disruption at a news conference worked well, but most often you won't have 100 supporters to help you chant. In general, the best way to deal with disruptions is to ignore them as long as possible and be polite and decent. You could even ask the disrupter to respond to a tough question. If you can't ignore heckling or disruptions, apologize to reporters and ask the disruptive person to calm down or leave. If he or she refuses, threaten to call the police and continue with the news conference. If you are asked obnoxious questions by "reporters" who may be your opponents, try to answer them and move on. If you suspect that people asking such questions are not really reporters, ask them to identify themselves and move on to other questions.

14

Alert the Media to Surprise Events and Civil Disobedience

SOME MEDIA EVENTS HAVE TO BE kept secret until the very last minute—or they might lose their impact or be made meaningless. Your event should not be publicized in advance if surprise is essential for its success. Your media strategy should be designed accordingly.

Sometimes activists want to catch officials in the act of doing something the activists feel is wrong. For example, citizens might receive a reliable tip that a public official is vacationing with lobbyists and want to catch him or her in the act. Or citizens might want to catch an official at a party with campaign contributors—without giving him or her the opportunity to prepare in advance for the confrontation. Similarly, activists dressed in chicken costumes may want to surprise an official with the accusation that he or she is afraid to tackle a tough issue.

Some acts of civil disobedience also rely on surprise. For example, if activists want to climb ancient trees to protest illegal logging, they must have access to the forest. If it's announced in advance that the activists are coming, officials may deny them access, effectively nixing the demonstration. The same surprise element is critical when activists protest housing policies by occupying vacant slum properties in the inner city, drop a huge banner from a building, or place in a meeting hall a briefcase that contains a taped message timed to "go off" during the meeting. All these actions of nonviolent civil disobedience rely on surprise.

Of course, some pranks of civil disobedience don't depend on surprise. For example, you wouldn't need a complex plan to alert the media to this recent act of civil disobedience: Activists with the Barbie Liberation Organization switched the voice boxes of Barbie and G.I. Joe dolls on sale at a toy store. Dressed in army fatigues and clad with machine guns and grenades, the G.I. Joe doll said, to the astonishment of the shopper who bought the item, "Want to go shopping?" and Barbie said in a deep voice, "Dead men tell no lies." This stunt got national media attention.

Nonviolent civil disobedience isn't just for lawless freaks. If it were, Mahatma Gandhi wouldn't be an international hero and Martin Luther King wouldn't have a national holiday in the United States named after him. Civil disobedience is a respected tool that activists use when they feel they must break the law—and when they are prepared to pay the possible consequences of jail time, fines, personal injury, and community disrepute.

Some may argue that attracting media attention to an act of civil disobedience cheapens its purity and transforms it into a manipulative stunt. I believe that media attention should be an integral part of serious civil disobedience. It simply expands the audience of witnesses to the injustice that's being opposed. As Bill Walker, a media trainer for the Ruckus Society, says: "The Quakers call it bearing witness—shining the light of public attention on injustice to bring about change. Work with the news media to bear witness more effectively to the widest audience."

Preparing for civil disobedience or a surprise demonstration is similar to organizing any media event (see Chapters 1–13). The major difference arises when you alert journalists to your event. This requires careful planning.

Tips for Alerting Journalists to
Surprise Media Events

• **Choose the proper location and time, compile a media list, and write a news release.**

Like any demonstration, a surprise protest should communicate one simple message, which should be reiterated on any signs, banners, or flyers prepared for the event. Similarly, the image of your protest—for example, of homeless families huddled in vacant housing—should be crafted to help communicate your simple message. Ideally your image should communicate your message without any verbal explanation.

Again, follow the regular principles of good media work. Your event, if possible, should occur earlier in the day (between 10 A.M. and 3 P.M.) and earlier in the workweek (Monday through Thursday). Your news release should be no more than one page with a dynamite headline and first paragraph. You should clearly state on it that video and photos are available. Here is the headline and first two paragraphs from a news release about an act of civil disobedience that occurred in Los Angeles. It was written by Bill Walker, who coordinated media outreach for the protest.

Burmese-Americans Block Unocal Truck
To Protest Company's Pipeline Project
[Photo and video available.]

A family of Burmese refugees chained themselves to a Unocal gasoline tanker early today to protest human rights abuses and rainforest destruction linked to construction of the LA-based company's southern Burma pipeline.

Dressed in traditional sarongs and holding their 4-year-old daughter, Maung and Taw Myo Shwe locked themselves to a truck leaving the Unocal Los Angeles Terminal Motor Transport facility at 13500 S. Broadway. They were joined by environmentalists from the International Rivers Network and other groups, who hung a large banner reading, "Unocal Stop Supporting the Brutal Burmese Regime."

• **Assemble your press kit.**

It should consist of about ten pages of background material neatly organized in a folder. It's a good idea to have a separate factsheet for distribution to the public, especially if you are engaging in civil disobedience in a public place.

• **Arrange to have a photographer and videographer at the event.**

Sometimes, if you fail to get journalists to attend your demonstration, you can later convince them to accept your photos or video of it. (Powerful news services like the Associated Press will accept photos occasionally. And broadcast outlets, including national and local news, may accept or even buy your video if it's good.)

You'll have a better chance of success if your photographer has some professional credentials as a freelancer, but this is not essential. For example, in British Columbia, activists failed to draw any media to their protest of the logging of the temperate rainforest. At their demonstration, which involved blocking a logging road with concrete barrels, workers from the logging industry vandalized cars, yelled at activists, chopped down a tree, and even started a fire near one activist who had chained himself to a barrel of concrete. Fortunately, the activists had a freelance videographer with them to tape the protest. After the event, the activists brought the film to local TV stations and received substantial—and lengthy—coverage on the evening news. The footage was accepted because it was so dramatic, showing the confrontation between the loggers and the activists.

• **Contact trusted journalists in advance.**

You'll probably get better media coverage if journalists know about your "secret" protest in advance, allowing them to plan to be on the scene. However, tipping off journalists is risky even if you tell them not to divulge your story to anyone in advance. Journalists may violate your "embargo" and thus undermine your protest. Or a journalist's editor might hear about it and alert the people you want kept in the dark. (A journalist might call someone from the opposing side for a comment on your upcoming event, inadvertently divulging your event.) You never know.

Your best bet is to give advance information about your surprise protest only to journalists whom you trust as professionals—and who will likely attend your demonstration. Call them and explain what's going to happen, where it will take place, and why you are asking them to keep it secret. It's best not to fax written information, which can get lost.

Depending on the complexity of your protest, you may decide to meet reporters at a specific location and lead them to your demonstration from there.

You may also decide—given the circumstances of your protest—to give advance warning to some reporters whom you do not know. One reason to do this: Your demonstration is in a remote location, making it impossible for them to get there on short notice. Another reason: You have to transport journalists on a boat or airplane to enable them to view your protest.

If you must tell unknown journalists in advance, call them directly if possible. If not, call city editors at newspapers, assignment editors at local television stations, producers at national shows, and news directors at radio stations.

Some activists opt to tell a larger number of journalists in advance that they have something planned without telling them the details or location. This helps them with planning, but it can be irksome to a reporter to receive partial information. I wouldn't recommend it unless your organization has an excellent track record.

- **Contact journalists when the demonstration begins.**

(In an ideal surprise protest, a few trusted journalists are on hand the instant your demonstration starts. You can contact more journalists by fax or e-mail and phone once the action begins.)

Station one person at the protest site and another in an office by a phone and fax machine. Once the action begins (e.g., activists have dropped a banner from the Statue of Liberty), your on-site person alerts the person in the office, who in turn faxes or e-mails your press release to all the reporters on your list.

Try to speed up the distribution of your news release. If possible, trigger your fax machine or e-mail distribution system from the demonstration site. Load your media list into your fax machine or computer in advance. It may be worth it to hire a service that will distribute faxes simultaneously to many journalists rather than your having to send them in succession. Bacon's Information, Inc., is one company that provides this service. (See Chapter 39, "Sources for Lists of News Outlets.") Any way to distribute your press release faster should be employed.

If you send faxes one at a time, prioritize the contacts on your list. Generally, wire services and television stations should be contacted first. But as with all media work, this depends on the audience you want to reach. Do your prioritizing according to which media outlet will best reach your target audience.

Call all journalists to make sure they've received your press release. (If you don't have a separate phone line for your fax machine, send one fax and then call right away. Then fax to your next highest priority and call, etc.) These calls are critical and should be practiced in advance. Get right to the point, emphasizing the drama and imagery of your demonstration.

Sample Call to a Journalist from a Surprise Media Event

Journalist: Associated Press.
You: I'm calling to let you know that two activists have just climbed the Sears Tower and dropped a huge banner down the side of the building that calls for an end to nu-

clear power. They're about 200 feet up the side of the Sears Tower right now.

Journalist: Do you have anything in writing?

You: I've just faxed you a press release, but I wanted to let you know that the protest is happening now at the Sears Tower. Did you receive the press release?

Journalist: I'll check. . . . Yes, I've got it. Can I reach you at this number?

You: Yes. Are you going to come down?

Journalist: I'll have to see. How long are you going to be there?

You: The police could remove us at any time. I'll keep you informed as the day goes on.

Journalist: Thank you.

Move through your list, making calls as quickly as you can, and then update journalists as the event proceeds. If major developments take place (confrontations, arrests, etc.), call key journalists again with updates. But don't pester anyone. If they don't sound interested, let them go quickly.

Use cell phones to call talk-radio programs from the action site. This live communication makes great radio news. In Chicago once, I was on a cell phone explaining to a television assignment editor at a local TV station that Greenpeace had two activists holding a banner on the side of a major hotel where nuclear power promoters were meeting. I said that the fire department was about to extract the activists from the side of the hotel. The fire truck had pulled up and the ladder was being extended toward the building. I asked the assignment editor if she was going to send anyone down. She said, "Call me if there is any blood or signs of police brutality." Clearly, local TV news in Chicago is tough to crack. But this protest would have been covered in most U.S. cities.

If your protest lasts days or weeks, expect coverage to accumulate over time. Don't get discouraged if you initially get no coverage. Your protest can provide a visual image for news that breaks while you're there.

When your demonstration ends, call all journalists who attended or expressed serious interest. Tell them what happened and where you can be reached during the rest of the day. If possible, conclude your protest with the media in mind. Sometimes you will want to negotiate an arrest scenario with police. If so, settle on a time for your arrest to coincide with live TV or before deadlines.

Finally, if you do get arrested, call journalists from jail. Talk-radio shows, in particular, are receptive to putting you on the air live from jail. (Plan for this by writing the phone number of media outlets on your body in case your clothes and belongings are taken from you.)

Sample Interactions with Media at an Event Involving Civil Disobedience

Sometimes during an act of civil disobedience, you will have time to answer only one question from a reporter. Your opportunity to deliver your sound bite may come as police are leading you to their patrol car and reporters converge on you.

Journalist: Why are you here?
You: I'm here to call on the U.S. government to ban mahogany imports.

Journalist: How do you go to the bathroom up in that tree?
You: Using diapers is inconvenient, but logging our old-growth forests would be a horrible tragedy.

Journalist: Do you have a job?
You: My job today is to alert citizens that the tobacco industry is killing our children by addicting them to cigarette smoking.

Journalist: Are you from this area?
You: It's everyone's responsibility to stop drunken driving.

Journalist: Do you care about putting workers out of their jobs?
You: We will have more jobs—and we'll save our forests—if we switch to tree-free products.

Everyone who attends your demonstration should practice delivering sound bites even if they don't plan to risk arrest or be involved in any way. Reporters will not focus exclusively on designated spokespeople. They want other "unpolished" points of view, which is fair enough. (This happened to my wife at a rally that I organized, and she got on national TV!) Everyone should be prepared to talk to a reporter. Some people may prefer to answer one or two questions and then tell a reporter to find the spokesperson.

15

Get Art Shows and Performances in the News

ARTISTS AND GALLERIES can get more news coverage than just an art review on page 54 of the weekend section. Artists should think as early as possible in their creative processes whether they want media coverage of their work or art show and, if so, create a newsworthy product. It's a lot easier to do this before creating art than to wait until the work is done. It might be easier for artists to approach their work this way if they think of themselves as activists as well as artists. Many activists consider the news value of their ideas before they undertake any project

Equating artists and activists isn't as big a leap as you might think. The stunts and demonstrations of Greenpeace, for example, have been interpreted by some critics as performance art. Dropping banners from buildings, from Mount Rushmore, or elsewhere could be considered more as public art "installations" than protests. Certainly, parading as whales or penguins is a kind of street theater.

The idea of activism being "art" is not new. Abbie Hoffman, the yippie media manipulator, described his media antics this way: "We would hurl ourselves across the canvas of society like streaks of splattered paint."[1]

By addressing social issues or public policy, artists often make their work newsworthy. They succeed by highlighting conflict or humor for the media. For example, Denver photographer Tory Read publicized an art show featuring photographs taken by

132

young people in a low-income, high-crime neighborhood. By informing journalists that the kids were "shooting back," she connected the exhibit to concerns about crime in the neighborhood. The art became a peaceful response to violence and received widespread coverage, including a piece on local TV news—highly unusual for an art show.

Read's exhibit, which took place in the community the artwork addressed, was also endorsed by neighborhood groups and civic leaders. This helped journalists accept it as an expression of community concern.

Other artists have recognized that forming a partnership with community leaders and groups can raise the news value of their work. When I worked for Greenpeace, a University of Colorado graduate student named Craig Freeman approached us with the idea of placing his art on twelve billboards that were sitting empty at the gates of Rocky Flats, a nuclear-bomb plant. He knew that Greenpeace was concerned about Rocky Flats, and in fact we had been inquiring about renting the billboards. We ended up forming a partnership in which we used his images and our words on six of the billboards and he retained complete control of the remaining six billboards for his work, which also related to Rocky Flats. It was a good deal for him because Greenpeace paid for all his materials and publicized the project, generating national media attention. (In an amusing twist that spawned interest by news media, another activist group protested Greenpeace's use of the billboards—even though they were at the gates of the nuclear-bomb factory—because billboards themselves are an environmental blight, or as one of the anti-Greenpeace activists put it, "Billboards are litter on a stick.") In any case, the partnership between Freeman, the artist, and Greenpeace, the community organization, proved effective in generating media attention.

Here's another example of how art was used in Greenpeace's campaign against Rocky Flats: I organized a Rocky Flats art show to highlight the environmental problems at the bomb plant. The show, which was widely covered by local TV news, took place at a time when Congress was cutting funds to the National Endowment for the Arts. My news release, which offered journalists convenient viewing times, featured this quote: "Perhaps Senator Jesse Helms would prefer that Denver artists paint pretty pictures of white sheep hopping around Mount Elbert. But fortunately local artists have other, more relevant, images in their minds. This art will allow citizens to attach images to their fears and concerns about—or perhaps their support for—Rocky Flats."

Other examples of media-friendly art—connected to current political issues—include Jenny Holzer's commercial-like word paintings (*Any Surplus Is Immoral*), Karen Finley's use of nudity and profanity to respond to Congress's arts cuts (attempts at censorship are almost always newsworthy), and the Guerrilla Girls posters.

If your art relates to a controversial issue, are you worried about your personal safety because of the content of your art show? About vandalism? You don't have to wait until your gallery, studio, or alternative art space is burned to make news. Your concerns about violence—if they are well founded—and the precautions you take could be newsworthy by themselves. Though not an arts organization, Planned Parenthood received wide coverage for erecting a fence around its abortion clinic to keep out protesters who were planning to rally there.

How Do For-Profit Businesses Attract Media Attention?

If you're a gallery owner or artist who would rather not address public policy issues in your work, you should look at how businesses publicize their activities in the mainstream media. Though you may see art as a cause in itself, most journalists see it as a private enterprise to be covered by the art reviewer, if there is one. So it's useful for you to look at examples of how private companies make news. (See Chapter 28, "Shine the Media Spotlight on Nonprofit Products.")

Many of the standard media tricks used by business are, in fact, used by arts promoters. Here are two examples:

- The ballet is in town, and the ballet promoters know they can't convince the TV news producers to run a story about their performance. The producers think it's boring. So the promoters arrange for some of the ballet stars to put on a short performance at an elementary school in a low-income neighborhood. The TV crews are waiting.
- A show by a well-known abstract artist is opening at a prestigious gallery, but—to no one's surprise—there is little media interest. So the gallery owners organize a free painting class, to be taught by the artist, for recovering alcoholics. This generates a large feature story.

To break out of the art-review section and into the news, you'll have to focus on different reporters and present different kinds of information about your exhibit than you would to an art reviewer. And you might have to abandon the gallery and show your art outside or in a more relevant location, which needs to be easily accessible for journalists. You'll also have to make the artwork available to journalists when it's convenient to them and execute your outreach to journalists correctly. (See Chapter 5, "Choose a Time to Maximize Coverage.") The usual opening reception on Friday night at the gallery won't cut it.

As always, think first about (1) why you want the attention of the news media and (2) which media will reach the audience you seek. Then develop a plan to reach your targeted media outlets.

Tips for Convincing a Critic to Review Your Show

Sometimes it's impossible to make art news. In fact, most often art isn't news and artists must settle for reviews. What's the best way to convince a critic to do a review?

- Don't work until the last minute on your art and think about the media once your show is hanging in the gallery. Develop a plan for media outreach at least one month before your show goes up.
- Make sure critics are aware of your show by calling them. As with outreach to other types of journalists, don't assume that a news release will be read. Call.
- If you are showing your work in a gallery, don't assume the gallery will do your media work for you. "A lot of times, galleries don't send out press releases, in which case artists should send an informative letter with salient information and slides of art work, not pictures of the artist," says Janet Tyson, visual art critic for the *Ft. Worth Star Telegram.*
- Don't bother critics. Once you're sure a critic knows about your show and has received your written materials, get off the phone.
- Make the work available to reviewers at convenient times. Reserve seats for journalists at productions.
- Don't get mad about a bad review. Critics are paid to tell us their opinions. Thank them for the review and perhaps discuss the work with them.
- Introduce yourself if you see a critic in a public place. A local artist who had just been panned by a local critic saw him at an opening and introduced herself, saying that everyone didn't always like her work. She chatted a bit with him. Ever since, he has religiously reviewed her work, most often favorably. "If people want to come up and introduce themselves, that's fine," says Janet Tyson at the *Ft. Worth Star Telegram.*
- If your work isn't reviewed, don't give up or get angry. As with other news, there's a lot of competition for limited space. Keep trying.

How to Get People to Attend Your Opening

Generating mainstream media coverage does not guarantee that more people will show up at your art opening. If your goal is to get people to attend your show, you should think about your larger marketing plan (e.g., who's the audience for your art and how will you reach them?). Usually, mailings to carefully selected lists and follow-up calls are the best way to convince people to come to an event. But media attention can definitely help.

16

Assess Your Media Event

AFTER YOUR MEDIA EVENT OCCURS, take time to discuss how it went. You should constantly evaluate all aspects of your media work.

Don't take it personally if your event receives scant coverage. It wasn't your fault that Mayor Blunder broke his leg tripping over a pothole. Remember, about 60 percent of the newspaper can be ads, and only a third of most local TV news shows is "news." And many radio stations are closing their news departments completely and laying off reporters.

Still, if you are shut out of the news, consider complaining. (See Chapter 35, "How and When to Complain About Coverage.") But don't assume that you didn't get covered because you're on a blacklist of unacceptable subjects. Whereas the ownership interests of media corporations can influence news coverage, the factors—including editorial staff—that combine to determine what's news at mainstream outlets change daily. Don't read Noam Chomsky's insightful ideas about self-censorship among journalists so closely that you end up giving up on the mainstream media. Chomsky himself wouldn't advocate this approach. Yes, the news media are increasingly concentrated in the hands of a decreasing number of corporations. But this does not necessarily mean you'll be excluded no matter how unconventional your views are.

Don't quit. As Juliet Whitman of the *Boulder Daily Camera* put it: "It's hard for a paper to ignore people who just don't give up."

Don't quit. Ongoing communications efforts will change the long-term direction of our society. Credit: Jason Salzman

If you succeeded in generating coverage, analyze it closely and identify ways to improve next time. Make sure you maximize the benefit from newspaper clips about your event, as described in the next section.

Tips for Maximizing the Benefit from News Coverage

- Even the most news-obsessed policy wonks don't see every article in the newspaper. Send all your "targets" (politicians, journalists, staff, executives, allies) your clips. This can create the illusion of a larger media event.
- Mail clips to donors, including foundations.
- Distribute clips within your own group.
- Extract quotes from articles—as politicians often do in election ads—to put in factsheets, brochures, and other documents for the general public. A quote from a newspaper article, no matter how insignificant the article, gives you legitimacy in the eyes of many people.
- Use clips in press packets at future events.
- Send tapes of TV interviews to important people and use the tapes in public outreach.

Remember that eight fleeting inches of ink in the daily newspaper can be next to worthless if it is not linked to a strategy for winning your campaign (e.g., reaching decisionmakers or a target audience). Think strategy first, media second.

Part Two

How to Generate News Coverage Without Staging a Media Event

CREATING A NEWS STORY through a media event, as described in Part 1 of this book, is one way to draw attention to your cause. But there are many other ways to use the news media for publicity.

The selection of which kind of "media work" to do depends on what you want to achieve. You may conclude that booking talk-radio appearances or publishing a guest opinion is more useful than organizing a media event.

Part 2 outlines how to suggest ideas for articles to feature writers and reporters and how to lobby editorial writers, columnists, and cartoonists. It gives you basic information on writing opinion articles and letters to the editor. It offers tips on injecting your cause into talk radio, community calendars, cable TV, and the Internet. It explains how to generate national and international news, how to publicize a report or academic paper, and how to get news coverage of a nonprofit product.

17

Suggest Ideas for News Stories to Journalists

D AY AFTER DAY, reporters are expected not only to write stories but to uncover them. They need your help. They want you to pitch them new information about an issue, and they want ideas about new ways to cover it. But they don't want to be pestered with irrelevant information or inane story ideas.

Your job is to know journalists and your issue well enough to give reporters what they need. If you do, you can play a significant role in shaping the debate about your cause. Pitching story ideas over the phone should be a priority of any publicist. It usually requires little time and can have a powerful impact.

"You can reach almost any journalist in America just by calling," says Michael Hirsh, a Washington, D.C., correspondent for *Newsweek*. "I'm looking for background information and ideas for stories," says Lorenz Wolf-Doettinchem, a correspondent for *Stern*, a German weekly magazine similar to *Newsweek* and *Time*.

Tips for Calling Journalists with Story Ideas

- Track your issue carefully in the news and note which reporters and news outlets seem to be most receptive to your information. Try them first. *"Dateline NBC* will look for a more in-depth story, while *Nightly News* is news of the day," says Ed Litvak, an assignment editor for NBC News. "There are certain stories that work for a morning audience that won't work for the evening."

- Think constantly about story ideas and scour your own sources for new information. Realize that journalists don't have the time you do to think about the progression of your issue. Your goal should be to stay ahead of the media with story ideas. Says Paul Day, a reporter for Denver's KCNC-TV, a CBS affiliate: "It's always helpful to be thinking a half week in advance. I shouldn't be starting a day from scratch."
- Ask yourself if your information or idea is of significant interest. Often we become so buried in our issues that we mistake insignificant changes for newsworthy developments. Remember that it's a reporter's job to evaluate and compare stories from different sources. "Some [organizations] have the attitude that their story is the only story in the world," says Craig Maclaine, a reporter for Radio Canada International.
- Suggest some stories that don't involve you and in which you would not expect to be quoted. This adds to your credibility.
- Offer story ideas gently. "There's nothing a journalist likes less than being told what to write," says Michael Hirsh at *Newsweek.* "Instead, say, 'I found out something interesting about ABC corporation in Indonesia.'"
- Remember that journalists don't just want information; they want stories.
- Don't request a meeting. It's too time-consuming for journalists.
- Ask if a reporter has a minute to talk. If so, lay out your idea in less than a minute, referring to visual elements if you are talking to a television journalist.

- Practice your pitch in advance.
- Think of ideas to get journalists out of the office. Sometimes they welcome the chance to get away from the desk for a half-day. A media-savvy biologist I met takes journalists into the field with him on research projects. Similarly—or not so similarly, I guess—police officials take journalists on raids.
- Be cognizant of how frequently you call a reporter. There is no rule about how often is too often because circumstances dictate different approaches. But don't overdo it.
- When you speak with a radio or TV journalist, remember that he or she is listening not only to what you say but to how you say it. You should look at your conversation as an audition for the show.
- When a journalist says, "I'm not interested," don't argue. Try again some other time with another idea. Just because a journalist rejected your idea once doesn't mean he won't like your next idea.

Exclusive Pitches

You can pitch a story to more than one journalist at a time. But often it makes more sense to offer a journalist an "exclusive," meaning that you will not give your story to any other journalists. (If you do this, consider whether giving an exclusive to one reporter can make other reporters angry with you.) If you decide to speak to only one reporter, make sure he or she knows that you are offering an exclusive. Your chances of being covered are better.

"I don't ask for exclusives," says Tom Lippman, a diplomatic correspondent at the *Washington Post*. "But I don't mind people saying to me, 'I'd like to see this story in the *Washington Post*. If you're interested in it, I won't shop it around. If you're not interested, let me know in forty-eight hours.'"

Sample News Story Pitch

Reporter: This is Joanne Reporter.

You: Hi, Joanne. It's Jerry Button from Save the Fish. If you have a minute, I thought I'd let you know about a development in the dead-sardines issue.

Reporter: Sure. Let's hear it.

You: You recall that sardines almost disappeared from the ocean around here in the 1980s. Congress enacted tough regulations. Well, the chief sardine weigher says more pounds of sardines have been caught this year than any year since 1982. The regulations, he says, seem to be working.

Reporter: You heard this from the chief sardine weigher?

You: Yes. I was at the dock and I stopped by the chief weigher's office.

Reporter: That's interesting. Who would've expected things to turn around so quickly?

You: That's what I thought. So I called Professor Fishhead. He told me that sardines are one of the fastest-reproducing fish on the planet. Given the chance, they do their thing quickly.

Reporter: Do you recall the name of the chief weigher you spoke with at the dock?

You: Yes. I've typed her name, a chronology, and other information for you. I'll fax it over.

Reporter: That would be great. I'll give her a call, check in with Professor Fishhead, and call you back. This looks like a good story.

You: I won't talk to anybody else about it. When do you expect to work on it?

Reporter: I've got time on Monday. I'll get back to you by the middle of next week.

You: I'll look forward to hearing from you.

Tips for Reacting to Breaking News

One of the easiest pitches is a reaction to breaking news. When a major story breaks, journalists are looking for comments from interest groups. Take advantage of this by offering them quotes from you.

"News is what is really happening," says Krystian Orlinski, an editor for Reuters Television, a news service. "You have to deal with things that are right there on the top of the agenda."

- Only react to breaking news that is clearly significant.
- Contact news reporters who you know cover day-to-day breaking news.
- If you call reporters, prepare your reaction quotes in advance and practice delivering them.
- If you fax or e-mail your reaction to reporters, keep the news release to about a half-page with a good headline and two quotes. (See Chapter 9, "Write a News Release.")
- Follow up any news release with a phone call. (See Chapter 12, "Call a Reporter After You've Sent a News Release.")
- Monitor CNN or news radio so you can hear about breaking news at about the same time print reporters do, allowing you to prepare quotes for the stories they are writing for the next morning's papers.
- Don't delay. You should get your reaction out the door as soon as you hear about the story, ideally before it hits the newspapers.

18

Pitch
a Feature Story

IT CAN BE MORE INTIMIDATING to pitch an idea for a feature story—a lengthy piece with human details and depth—than a news story, which is generally shorter with a factual focus. "News" has some defining characteristics even if they're amorphous. But features are harder to define than news. After all, what's feature-worthy? In the hands of a good writer, anything can be a feature. Even my mom can be a subject for a feature story. In fact, she's been one. So how does a feature writer decide what to cover in a world spilling over with potential feature articles?

The answer is this: Like other journalists, feature writers cover what they hear about or stumble across—or what their editors tell them to write about. If feature writers stumble across you (with your assistance), you can help them think of subjects for articles—just as you might help a news reporter think of news stories.

Feature writers are looking for good story ideas, and they want to hear from you, especially if your idea matches their interests. "Do your research," says Colin Covert, a feature reporter for the *Star Tribune* in Minneapolis. "Tailor your story to the tastes of individual reporters."

Tips for Generating a Feature Story

- At a newspaper, feature stories are written both by news reporters and by designated feature writers. You can pitch feature ideas to both.
- Develop contacts with feature writers. As with other media outreach, contacts help and should be cultivated, but they are not essential.
- If your feature idea relates to an event, pitch it to feature reporters at least two weeks before the event.
- You don't need to write a news release to generate a feature. In fact, having one can turn some reporters off to your story idea.
- Have written information or background video ready. In some cases, a short e-mail or letter followed by a phone call can be productive, especially because it's hard to catch feature writers on the phone, and they may not return your phone calls. Colin Covert at the *Star Tribune* suggests sending a postcard before calling: "With a postcard, maybe with something funny on it, I don't even have to open it. If you've got the right pitch, you ought to be able to fit it on a postcard."
- In pitching feature stories by phone, follow the professional protocol that you would with other journalists: Respect deadlines. Get right to the point. Practice your pitch.
- In many cases, you'll want to work exclusively with one journalist on a feature story. Use common sense to decide when exclusivity is necessary.
- Radio and television outlets air fewer features than print outlets. But as the line between entertainment and news vanishes, broadcast news outlets air more features. With the right idea and the right visual punch, your feature might be useful for a TV news magazine, local TV news, or national news. On local TV news, "soft news"—which

could include your feature story—is one of the top subjects behind disaster and crime.

- When you are trying to convince journalists to accept your feature topic, don't limit yourself to staff journalists. Freelance writers are also looking for good ideas. You should collect names of freelance journalists. Call the freelancers who work for a news outlet that might be appropriate for your feature story.

19

Lobby
Editorial Writers

THE OFFICIAL POSITIONS of a newspaper are found in its editorials, which are unsigned opinions usually printed beneath the paper's name and vital statistics—the editor's name, the publisher's name, and so on. (These are *not* the signed opinion pieces in the paper by local and national pundits. For information on influencing these opinion columnists, see Chapter 22, "Convince a Columnist to Write About Your Issue.")

The masses don't read editorials, but policy wonks, community leaders, and other governmental types devour them. Sometimes they're quoted in ads (e.g., the *Idaho Statesman* says . . .). Depending on your goals, it can be worthwhile to convince a newspaper that your opinion should be its position. You do this by lobbying editorial page staff.

Each newspaper has its own process for making decisions about the content of editorials. At many newspapers, the publisher—in consultation with an "editorial board"—is technically in charge of deciding which editorials are printed and what positions the newspaper advocates in them. This board may consist of the paper's editor, editorial page editor, and others.

In practice, the editorial page editor and editorial writers usually make most decisions relating to editorials unless a high-profile issue such as the endorsement of a major political candidate is involved. At larger newspapers, editorial writers are assigned issue areas (e.g., education and the environment) and are responsible for writing the paper's editorials on those issues.

At many newspapers, such as the *Cleveland Plain Dealer* and *Seattle Times*, the editorial writers and editors meet each morning to discuss editorials. These journalists present ideas for editorials and analyze both sides, often playing devil's advocate with one another. They strive for consensus.

"The writer makes the case to the rest of the staff about what the position of the paper should be," says Jim Vesely, associate editorial page editor of the *Seattle Times*. "Often, but not always, the writer's position prevails."

Most editorials are written two to three days in advance of publication, but sometimes they can be written a week or more in advance. Editorial writers are usually working on a weekend piece on Wednesday or Thursday. On Friday, they're writing a Monday piece.

As you interact with editorial page staff, keep their deadlines in mind and be aware of how busy they are. "Just as we understand that groups want to be heard, they have to understand that we are inundated with requests to meet with us," says Brent Larkin, editorial page director of the *Cleveland Plain Dealer*.

Tips for Initiating Contact
with Editorial Page Staff

- First, familiarize yourself with the position the newspaper has taken on your issue in the past.
- Then, call. Dial the main number of a newspaper and ask for the editorial page. "I prefer an initial contact by phone, followed up by a letter or e-mail," says Jim Vesely at the *Seattle Times*.
- Ask to speak with the editorial writer who specializes in your issues. Large metropolitan dailies may have five editorial writers plus the editorial page editor. A smaller pa-

per may have only one. "Don't be hesitant to pick up the phone and give us a call," says Vincent Carroll, editorial page editor of the *Rocky Mountain News*, adding that "persistence pays."

- Once you've hooked the right person on the phone, briefly explain your position and ask if he or she would like to (1) receive information by mail or e-mail, (2) talk more on the phone, or (3) arrange a meeting. "Sometimes we'll invite people to come in, and sometimes we'll ask for written material," says Brent Larkin at the *Cleveland Plain Dealer*.

List of Written Information for Editorial Page Staff

- A one-page summary of your position, including details such as complete titles of laws, phone numbers of experts, numbers of people or acres involved, quantity of materials, and other relevant statistics.
- Newspaper articles.
- One feature article or a summary of a report.
- Previous editorials that relate to your issue.
- No more than ten pages of credible, concise information. (Follow up with a phone call the subsequent week to find out if more material is needed.)

Tips for Calling Editorial Page Staff

- Like other journalists, editorial writers are busy. You need to pitch your opinion to them quickly.
- Ask if they have a moment to talk.
- Be aware of deadlines. Usually the beginning of the week is better than the end to establish contact.

- Be concise. Answer questions directly.
- Ask what they need from you.
- Send a follow-up note with written information (see the previous list).
- If they disagree with your position, suggest that they publish a guest opinion written by you or someone who shares your perspective. (See Chapter 20, "Write a Guest Opinion.")

Tips for Meeting with Editorial Page Staff

A meeting is the exception rather than the rule, as meetings are usually reserved for new, complex issues or major recent developments (or for Senator Roundhead, who's in town). If you have a meeting, you'll likely sit down with an editorial writer and possibly the editorial page editor. "For a bigger topic, we'll bring in six or seven people plus the publisher," says Jim Vesely at the *Seattle Times*.

- Conduct a ten-minute practice session before the meeting, responding to difficult questions. (It helps to know something about previous editorial positions.)
- Take no more than four people. Well-known experts with credentials are great as long as they can explain their views simply.
- Don't expect more than a half-hour.
- Bring the same written materials you would have sent had there been no meeting (see "List of Written Information for Editorial Page Staff").
- Leave videos at the office.
- Offer to submit an op-ed if the editors do not adopt your position. (See Chapter 20, "Write a Guest Opinion.")
- Write a follow-up note offering further information.

Responding to an Error in an Editorial

Editorial writers are usually around longer than politicians; consequently, you should avoid destroying long-term relationships over errors or differences of opinion. If an error is made, call the editorial writer, set the facts straight, and send sources of accurate information. He or she may advise you to submit a letter to the editor, which may make sense depending on the gravity of the mistake.

"Everyone will pick up the paper sometimes and feel it's wrong," says editorial writer Steve Millard at the *Boulder Daily Camera*. "But keep criticism from reaching the point of hostility."

Over the long term, keep editorial writers informed, but don't bury them in paper. It's probably not worth sending ongoing publications such as newsletters to editorial page writers unless they request them. If you do send such information to local newspapers, it should probably address regional or local issues. Writers say they may "scan" or "glance at" newsletters.

20

Write a Guest Opinion

Publishing a guest opinion in the newspaper helps legitimize both your cause and you as a knowledgeable spokesperson for it. Also, a published opinion may turn out to be an excellent position paper for distribution to policymakers, the public, and funders.

These opinion pieces are commonly called op-eds because they're typically published opposite the editorial page. The op-ed page may also contain columns by the paper's regular columnists and by nationally known writers. The latter are distributed electronically to papers across the country; thus your op-ed could run alongside Pat Buchanan's.

Some papers accept opinion columns for publication in other sections of the newspaper, such as the business section. Keep an eye open for these opportunities.

To submit an op-ed, call the newspaper and ask for the editor of the op-ed page. This is the person who decides, sometimes with other editors' input, which opinion columns appear in the paper. Some editors don't encourage calls from writers they do not know, especially at newspapers like the *Boston Globe* and *USA Today*, which receive about 100 unsolicited op-eds per week and publish only a handful. But you should call them anyway, making sure to be polite and aware of deadlines. The best time to call is early in the week and early in the day.

Once you get through, which may take repeated calls, describe the gist of your piece and ask if the editor would like to take a look at it. Although it's impossible for an editor to accept a piece without seeing it, he or she will usually be able to tell you if you are duplicating other efforts or if there's any interest at all. Your call may prompt him or her to organize a pro/con forum on your issue.

"I encourage writers to work something up two to three weeks before an event," says Glen Nishimura, op-ed page editor for *USA Today.* "Anticipate news. Don't just react to it. I've got a game plan for many events."

If you've got relevant credentials, send a copy of your resume with your submission, which can be mailed, faxed, or, possibly, e-mailed. Also write a brief cover letter reminding the editor of your phone conversation. You can send your piece to two or three different papers at the same time, but make sure you indicate in your cover letter that you are doing so.

Many newspapers will send you a letter only if your op-ed is accepted. If you don't hear anything a week after submitting your op-ed, call to make sure it was received.

Tips for Writing Op-Eds

- Aim for 700 words—no more than 1,000—and double-space.
- Write in the active voice with two- to three-sentence paragraphs.
- Try not to be ponderous. "Write op-eds in an anecdotal or story-telling way," says Glen Nishimura at *USA Today.*
- Focus on local or regional angles for local newspapers and on broader topics for national papers. "We're looking for things that go beyond the predictable and relate to trends in a variety of communities," says Nishimura at *USA Today.*
- It's more likely your op-ed will be accepted if your view is different from the newspaper's editorial position. "On op-

eds, we give preference to people who disagree with us,"
says Jim Vesely, associate editorial page editor at the *Seattle Times*.

- Respond to specific newspaper stories with a letter, not an op-ed.
- Put your name, phone, and address in the top left-hand corner.
- Type the number of words in the upper right-hand corner.
- Give it a short title.
- Type "—30—" or "—end—" at the bottom of the last page and "more" at the bottom of all other pages.
- Editors say that just before the holidays and toward the end of summer are good times to submit op-eds because there is less competition. However, as a rule, you should write a piece when your issue is timely.

Sample Op-Ed

Jason Salzman   600 words
Rocky Mountain Media Watch
Box 18858
Denver, CO 80218
303-832-7558

Activism Should Be Seen as a Profession

The essential task of political activists—from antiabortionists to disarmers—is to prod citizens to engage in politics.

With the world's problems mounting and political apathy growing, activists are needed now, more than ever, to convince people to become part of the collective solutions to global and local ills. Activists, who may represent causes on the left or right of the political spectrum, are needed to nurture the emergence of our nearly nonexistent political culture.

Despite the apparent truism, political activism and even the word "activist" carry little, if any, legitimacy in our society. To make political activism a more acceptable activity, now is the time to recognize it as a profession.

To do this, it must be made clear that activists are not simply a band of time-warped hippies or the idle rich. Activists are not all desperate, overworked missionaries—so laden with personal problems that they cannot find work in the "for-profit" world. They are not constantly tilting at windmills—though sometimes this is a necessity—or singing folk songs.

Instead, an increasing number of "activists" and workers in the nonprofit sector are qualified professionals who make a livable income doing something they think is important. Like other professionals, these activists work long but reasonable hours, enjoy their work, and try to apply their skills creatively.

If activism is to be considered a profession, even a lowly one, it also must be recognized that the work of an activist involves skills that take time to develop, though they are often learned on the job rather than in ivory towers.

An activist develops sophisticated public relations skills, including an ad designer's sense of slogans and imagery and an ability to communicate with all elements of society. By the nature of their work, activists develop the skills of fund-raisers, lawyers, researchers, journalists, graphic artists, mediators, scientists, accountants, and teachers. And if nonviolent civil disobedience is required, they are suddenly "criminals," too.

Currently, activism has no ranking as a profession. Activists have no national professional societies, no trade journals, and few professional awards—all of which should be established or augmented. Activism is not even considered on a par with other professions acquired largely through apprenticeship, such as journalism or cooking.

At best, activism is seen as nothing more than a pit stop on the way to a job involving more money, less time, and more real influence.

With undervalued skills and unappreciated importance, activists are sometimes severely underpaid, leading them to burn out and quit. Part of the blame for this must be placed on nonprofit organizations, which in many cases should hire fewer staff at higher pay.

A contributing factor to the social delegitimization of activism is that the traditional tactics of activists (e.g., rallies, letter-writing campaigns, vigils, even voter-registration drives) are seen as either ineffective or appropriate only for the 1960s. This has left many citizens with no clue—much less desire—about how to affect politics in our troubled democracy.

Ironically, to solve this crisis of democratic expression, we need more activists with professional credibility—regardless of political affiliation—to convince citizens that the traditional and nontraditional tactics of activists, if utilized, are effective and appropriate.

Recognizing activism as a profession would in no way mean that the nonprofessional activist, who is mad as hell about the toxic dump in town, should become a professional activist or shut up. On the contrary, professionals are needed to help sustain the energy of these people—and to help recruit others to become involved.

Jason Salzman is the author of *Making the News: A Guide for Nonprofits and Activists.*

—end—

21

Publish
a Letter to the Editor

THE LETTERS PAGE, which is located in the commentary section of the newspaper, has wide appeal to both policymakers and citizens. In fact, many journalists say readers like the letters page more than any other section of the newspaper.

"Letters are very well read," says Marjorie Prichard, op-ed page editor for the *Boston Globe*, adding that groups that focus only on op-eds do themselves a "disservice." "Letters reflect the community. People read the letters page."

In any case, it's a lot easier to publish letters to the editor than longer guest opinions, which frequently appear across from the letters page. Most local dailies don't run many op-eds by ordinary citizens, and there's keen competition for the limited space available. At the national level, it's even more difficult to publish an op-ed because most guest columns are reserved for well-known writers or officials. "Groups have a much better chance of getting a letter in than an op-ed," says Brent Larkin, editorial page director at the *Cleveland Plain Dealer*.

Some newspapers reserve space for letters not only in the editorial or commentary section but also in other sections of the newspaper, such as the business section. Take advantage of all opportunities to publish letters.

Tips for Writing Letters to the Editor

- Find out the guidelines for letters to the editor. Most papers set a 100–200 word limit for letters.
- Generally, stick to the word limit because it's better that you're in control of what gets cut from your letter than a faceless editor. But also realize that many longer letters appear in print. Try to assess realistically the importance of your letter.
- Write in short paragraphs.
- Put your full name, address, and phone number at the top of the letter and sign it at the bottom.
- Don't submit form letters.
- Send letters by e-mail, fax, or regular mail.
- Write in the summer, when there's less competition.
- Read the letters page. You'll know if your brilliant idea occurred to someone else first, and you'll develop an effective letter-writing style.
- Avoid personal attacks.
- Compose your letter with the assumption that readers know nothing about your topic.
- Your letter has the best chance of being published if it's a reaction to a story in the paper. Respond as quickly as you can to the story by e-mail or fax if either is accepted. If not, you might deliver the letter by hand.
- Don't assume your idea will be rejected. Most papers don't blacklist ideas.
- Respond directly to other letters to the editor. But you should know that editors usually cut off an ongoing debate on the letters page at some point.
- Don't write too frequently. There's no rule applicable to all papers, but once every three months is probably about as often as you should write.
- After about ten days, you can call to find out why your letter has not appeared.

Sample Letter to the Editor

Jason Salzman
Rocky Mountain Media Watch
Box 18858
Denver, CO 80218
303-832-7558

January 10, 1998

Letters to the Editor
Newspaper
10 Silver Plume Lane
Motown, CA 94102

Dear Editor:

Congratulations on your decision (5/25/97) to add a weekly column written by a member of our community.

Most everyone appreciates a good sampling of elite punditry. Nationally known columnists generally have lots of experience and connections. But if you're a close pundit watcher, you know that—even though their opinions differ—regular columnists do not add the breadth of diversity that guest writers bring to the opinion pages. Regular pundits observe society from similar, if not identical, places. After all, they're all high-profile pundits.

Guest writers, in contrast, have different jobs and spheres of activity. They don't look at the world and see a column. You could offer more balance on your opinion pages by reserving space for a handful of guest columns each week—and still leave plenty of room for regular pundits.

Sincerely,

Jason Salzman
President

22

Convince a Columnist to Write About Your Issue

NEWSPAPERS HIRE COLUMNISTS to write opinions—not the paper's opinion, not your opinion, but the columnists' personal opinions. They do not hire columnists to write fair, balanced articles. Reporters are supposed to do this. The job of a columnist is to comment on "issues" in some way, sometimes satirically, sometimes whimsically, sometimes—unfortunately for us—unintelligibly. Columnists may write monthly, weekly, or four times a week.

Most columnists develop a particular style of writing that becomes familiar to readers over time. They also often write repeatedly about a set of issues or themes, and their opinions on these issues are frequently predictable.

Learn the Interests and Styles of Local Columnists

Read as many pieces by local columnists as you can endure, including those that appear in alternative papers. Identify the columnists who—based on their work—might have an interest in your cause. Then offer them ideas for columns suited to "their issues" and style of writing.

"I solicit readers' input," says Peter Rowe, a columnist for the *San Diego Union*. "I love it. Yesterday, I heard from someone and

I'll be meeting with him and following up on the story tomorrow."

"I'm open to listening to people, as long as they don't have some hare-brained concept that has no base in reality," says Kirk Knox, a columnist for the *Wyoming Tribune-Eagle*.

Tips for Pitching Story Ideas to Columnists

- Call columnists on the phone. Have written information ready to fax or mail if the columnist is interested.
- Save your time and theirs by contacting only columnists who might write about an issue like yours.
- On the phone, be brief. Practice your pitch in advance. You should know within a couple of minutes whether the columnist is interested.
- Don't ask for a lunch date. "A lot of times people want to meet with you," says Peter Rowe at the *San Diego Union*. "I don't have a lot of time for meetings."
- You can write a one-page letter with your idea. Address the envelope by hand to help ensure that it gets opened amid the sea of junk mail columnists receive. Follow up with a phone call within a week.
- Most columnists will not conduct an in-depth investigation on your behalf—primarily because they have too many columns to write and little time and no staff for investigation.
- Columnists will seldom give your group's event—such as a benefit race—free publicity. But be on the lookout for "society" columnists who specifically plug events. You'll see in the paper that they mention community events in their columns.
- Make sure you know if the columnist you want to contact is local or national. Most columns in local newspapers are written by nationally syndicated writers whose work ap-

pears in many papers. Look at the end of the column for a tag identifying the columnist. (Think about pitching an idea to a national columnist if you've got a unique story.)

- Consider contacting a columnist who you know disagrees with you about your cause and writes about it frequently. An angry column opposing your position can sometimes kick up a local debate that you will eventually win.

Tips for Keeping Columnists Informed

- If a column contains inaccurate information, call or write a columnist and present documented, correct information. But remember, it's not a columnist's job to present both sides of a debate. Be reasonable. Remember that columnists are people—not institutions—with whom you should try to develop a respectful relationship. There's a good chance they will be writing columns for many years, outlasting politicians and the day's "hot" issue.

- Columnists don't track breaking news like a reporter—so avoid sending them press releases—but they might be interested to know about a visiting speaker whom they might interview.

- Generally, don't send more than a couple of pages of information to a columnist. "People think the way to get into the paper is to overwhelm us with information," says Gene Amole, a columnist at the *Rocky Mountain News*. "That just doesn't work. . . . No one has time to read that stuff."

- Some columnists like to receive newsletters, particularly if they are directly related to issues they write about frequently. Keep in mind that columnists toss most newsletters immediately.

- If a columnist tells a story and pieces of it are left out, let him or her know what's missing. A columnist may come back to your topic later.

- Though a big plus, personal relationships are not essential in convincing a columnist to write about your cause. "I've got to say, my mother keeps giving me story ideas, and I rarely use them," says Peter Rowe at the *San Diego Union.* "And she is a bright, capable person."

23

Influence Newspaper Photographers

DON'T LEAVE NEWSPAPERS' photo departments in the dark-room. Unlike television journalists, whose medium demands that they constantly think about imagery to accompany their stories, reporters at newspapers don't necessarily make quality photos a priority. Reporters or editors may reject a press release about an event that lacks "news value" without considering carefully whether the event merits a photo.

You can make sure the "photo considerations" of your event are fully weighed by sending press releases—or an idea for a photo—to the photo departments at newspapers. At larger papers, contact the photo assignment editor. Follow up a fax or a letter with a phone call. "There is no problem with people calling photo departments directly," says Dave Einsel, director of photography for the *Houston Chronicle*. "I don't mind phone calls. I like interacting with the public. It makes life fun."

How Do Photos Get in the Newspapers?

Reporters and other newspaper staff request photographs to accompany stories they're writing. The photo editor evaluates the requests and assigns the photographers.

Sometimes, however, the photo department does not receive enough requests from the news department because communication breaks down—which can happen at any large company—or the shots requested don't make good photographs. The photo department then looks for other photo opportunities. That's why it needs to know about your events and ideas. Contact the photo editor or individual photographers by fax one to three days prior to your event. Place your follow-up phone call when photographers are the least busy: early in the day, Monday through Thursday, or on Sunday morning before the sports events. (Also see Chapter 5, "Choose a Time to Maximize Coverage.") "If we've got nothing else to do, nothing is too stupid," says Dave Einsel at the *Houston Chronicle.* "It's our job to take pictures."

Don't treat photographers like they're photo machines or appendages of a reporter. Sometimes they write a piece as well as shoot the event. If you insult their intelligence, it's not as likely that you'll find a photo of your event in the paper, much less a good one.

Develop a relationship with photographers. Like any other journalists, they can be influenced, and they have the power to suggest shots to their editors. Also, a photo editor or photographer can suggest stories to reporters. "It doesn't hurt to put a photographer who expresses an interest on your mailing list," says Brian Brainerd, a photographer for the *Denver Post.*

24

Sway a Cartoonist

BEING A CARTOONIST is kind of a lonely job," says Mike Smith, cartoonist for the *Las Vegas Sun*. "You're kind of a hermit in the far reaches of the newsroom. You're bound up in a room and in your mind. There are so many days I get cabin fever and I'd just like to go outside and walk around. . . . It's nice to know what people are thinking. It's useful to get a perspective of people who are reading the paper, not just the perspective of an editor. It's good to find out what people outside the newsroom are thinking."

Cartoonists at newspapers should hear from you. If a picture is worth a thousand words, a cartoon can be worth millions of them—and a cartoon can be reprinted in a small space and distributed to decisionmakers, supporters, and opponents.

Tips for Lobbying Cartoonists

Cartoonists want information directly related to what's in the news. They deal with what's very current. You'll notice that most cartoons are simple responses to events. Therefore, it's not useful to send detailed or esoteric information to cartoonists.

Give information to a cartoonist that highlights an irony or contradiction. This helps cartoonists because, as you can see from reading cartoons, many cartoons highlight paradoxes.

Tell cartoonists what's going to happen related to your issue. They want tips on upcoming events—hearings, visits by officials.

"A reminder of an event [such as national Stop Smoking Week] might be a nudge," says Tom Toles, cartoonist for the *Buffalo News*. Cartoonist Ed Stein of the *Rocky Mountain News* recalls that numerous employees of the Environmental Protection Agency despised former EPA administrator Ann Gorsuch. Some of these EPA officials would tell Stein when Gorsuch was coming to Denver and give him details of the administrator's policies. He would have a cartoon ready for the paper when she was in town. (Cartoonists, who may draw six cartoons a week at a metropolitan daily, frequently draw pieces the day before publication.)

"I do want to hear from people if they disagree," says *Denver Post* cartoonist Mike Keefe, acknowledging that this may affect future cartoons. For Keefe, responses are important because he sees discussion about cartoons as advancing, in a "small way," the debate about public policy.

Don't offer specific ideas for a cartoon. Cartoonists don't want creative help—just information. "People get a thorn in their side and they call," says Smith at the *Las Vegas Sun*. "Everyone's got the Pulitzer Prize–winning cartoon. . . . I don't think I've ever used an idea from someone who's called."

Complain to a cartoonist about cartoons based on inaccurate information. At that point, give the cartoonist the facts over the phone—and send a follow-up letter with documentation.

On occasion, let a reporter or an editorial writer know that a piece was "fair and accurate." But don't try this on a cartoonist. Cartoonists want to have the facts straight, but unlike for reporters, professional standards don't demand that they be fair.

Read a cartoonist's work in the paper and send information that's related to the topics that seem to interest her most. Cartoonist Toles at the *Buffalo News* says: "Personally, I tend to pay attention to environmental suggestions because it's of interest to me and it's an area that's underreported."

25

Tune Your Cause
to Talk Radio

TALK RADIO can be a political and social force. It attracts a de-
voted band of listeners, particularly older people who are active
in their communities and vote. If you've got the right subject and
an articulate spokesperson, you should use talk radio's shows to
get your message out.

Before calling radio stations, save your own time and the time
of the talk-show staff by learning which programs might air an issue like yours. Listen to as much talk radio as you can without
going crazy. Different shows focus on different themes—sports,
health, current affairs, astrology, cars, and much more.

"If it has nothing to do with sports or entertainment, we're not
interested," says Leonard Nelson, producer of KNBR-AM radio's
morning show in San Francisco. "We want stuff that will keep
them going in the morning."

"Do some research," advises David Lauer, producer of the *Mike
Rosen Show* for Denver's KOA-AM radio. "I get many offers for
guests that just don't have a chance."

Tips for Booking a Guest on Talk Radio

- Once you've identified an appropriate show for your issue, call the radio station and ask for the name of the producer of that show.

- Call the producer and pitch your guest and topic. (See "Sample Call to a Talk-Radio Producer" in this chapter.) Make your call a month in advance if possible, but programs sometimes need guests on the spur of the moment.
- If you know a host personally, call him or her directly. At some smaller stations, contact the host directly whether or not you're acquainted. Be concise.
- Try not to leave a message on voice mail, and if you do use voice mail, say, "Please call" rather than "Call if you're interested."
- If the producer or host is interested in your idea, mail or fax a one-page description of your topic and guest.
- The producer may book the guest right away or discuss the booking with the host and get back to you. "We think about whether it will reach our target audience," says Leonard Nelson at KNBR radio.
- If the producer is not interested, take no for an answer and say good-bye without dragging out the conversation or becoming confrontational. "Losing gracefully is appreciated," says Lauer at KOA radio. "I'll be more receptive next time they call."
- It's not worth sending your group's informational publications to talk shows. Stick to pitching specific subjects and guests to producers and hosts.
- You've got a better chance at booking a guest in the summer, which tends to be a slower time of year. The week after Christmas can also be slow.

Tips for Talk-Radio Interviews

- Any show—even if it has a hostile host—can be a good opportunity to publicize your issue. But don't book a mediocre spokesperson on any show.

- Become familiar with the host and the format of the show in advance.
- Your voice will sound much better if you're interviewed from the studio rather than from a phone. You'll be kept on the air longer, too.
- Tell your supporters to call the show when you're on the air, especially if you expect to face a belligerent host.
- Ask a friend to tape the show so that you can critique your performance later.
- Arrive at the station a few minutes early.
- Bring some notes with you, but don't read a statement.
- If you have a dynamite audio piece available, bring it to the station and ask that it be played on the air.
- Warm up your body and your voice before you go on the air. Babble for a few minutes or sing. Loosen your facial muscles. Stretch as if you were going jogging.
- Ask for headphones.
- Once you're in the studio, get to know the host. Chat during commercial breaks and prior to going on the air. But refrain from talking about your subject with the host in the studio. You may forget once you're on the air what you've already covered in the studio.
- Announce your organization's name and phone number on the air.
- Don't answer questions with a simple yes or no. Explain your position and have an exchange with the host.
- Summarize numbers. For example, say "just over a third" instead of "33.9 percent."
- Use vocal inflections and avoid "ah" and "ahm." Clarity, emotion, and intensity make good talk radio. (Check out the movie *Talk Radio* for a depressing, if overly dramatic, look into the emotional world of talk radio.)
- Talk at a natural speed. Especially avoid speaking toooo sloooowly.

- Get angry only if you've made a rational decision that it's the right tactic. If your host is quarrelsome, try humor as an antidote. Don't be defensive.
- Ask the host questions. This makes the interview more conversational and takes away the momentum from a host who is attacking you.
- Don't be hesitant to speak over a caller. Many stations have technology that allows your voice to come through over a caller's.
- Try to achieve an intimacy on talk radio, as if you're talking one-on-one to a friend.

Sample Call to a Talk-Radio Producer

You: Hello, I'm Jason Salzman, author of *Making the News*, a book about how citizens can break into the news with stories about issues that concern them.

Producer: Can you hold on a second. . . . Yes, excuse me. You were saying?

You: My book argues that citizens shouldn't just complain about the news. I offer information—

Producer: That's nice. Everybody complains about the news. It's like the weather, constant complaints.

You: I complain about the weather every day even if it's good weather, but I can't do anything about it. But citizens can do something about the news by making their own. That's what my book is about. How people can gain access to the news—editorials, newspaper stories, television, talk radio—all the news. They can shine the media spotlight on issues that concern them.

Producer: Most people prefer to complain about the news than make their own.

You: I agree. But I've noticed that a theme on your show is discussing how people can act on their own, take matters into their own hands, that kind of thing. Our discussion could revolve around the question "Can ordinary citizens break into the news?" I believe they can.

Producer: That's interesting. We've had a lot of news critics on the show, and none of them has made that argument. So your book is a how-to-make-news manual?

You: Yes, exactly—for nonprofits, activists, or anyone with a cause.

Producer: Do you have a description?

You: Yes, I'll fax it over now.

Producer: I'll take a look at it, talk to Mike, and get back to you.

You: Thanks for your time.

26

Place Your TV Production
or Information on Cable

THE COMMUNITY ACCESS CENTER in Kalamazoo, Michigan, broadcasts a program—called *Doggy in the Window*—produced by a local animal shelter. Dogs available for adoption are presented on the show. The Community Access Center doesn't charge the animal shelter anything to air the program on a cable access channel or to use the equipment necessary to produce it. Since *Doggy in the Window* hit the cable wire, the shelter's adoption rate for dogs has doubled.

Community Access Television of Salina, Kansas, places a notice—submitted by a local food bank—on its televised community bulletin board that a specific food item is needed. The food bank has to run a second notice, stating that it has all of that particular kind of food that it can handle.

If cable television is available in your area, it's likely that at least one cable channel—called the public access channel—broadcasts information from citizens and nonprofit organizations. Most public access channels air announcements about nonprofit events and services. They also broadcast independently produced TV programs and even offer classes on how citizens can produce their own TV show. Once trained, citizens can create and broadcast their own TV program using the access channel's equipment.

Most staff at public access channels around the country are eager to help citizens and nonprofits. "We're in the business of facilitating the public and nonprofit use of the [cable access] channels by training people to create television productions," says Roxanne Earnest, administrative coordinator for Community Access Television of Salina, Kansas. "In essence, it's communication of, by, and for the public."

What Is Cable Access?

Cable television consists of multiple TV channels that are wired into people's homes on a thick wire or cable. Citizens in most metropolitan areas can buy access to cable television by calling the local cable operator and arranging for the wire to be connected to their homes. Once installed, cable television increases the number of channels on a television set by dozens or, potentially, by hundreds or more. Cable usually improves TV reception as well.

Cable operators such as TCI or Cablevision offer TV viewers cable "packages." A viewer can buy, say, a dozen channels for about $25 per month. For a higher price, a hundred channels may be available, and so on. Different cable packages include different mixes of well-known cable channels such as Arts and Entertainment (A&E), Cable News Network (CNN), Cable National Broadcasting Company (CNBC), Nickelodeon, Discovery, the Learning Channel, the Shopping Network, Music Television (MTV), movie channels, weather channels, sports channels, and foreign language channels. Some cable packages also offer viewers the capability to pay for movies and events on a pay-as-you-view-them basis. Viewers let the cable operator know in advance that they want to watch a program on pay-per-view, and the cable operator then sends it to them over the cable. Cable operators must carry the local TV stations' signals as well.

Installing the network of wires for cable television in a city is a major public works project, much like installing telephone lines, making it essentially impossible for more than one cable operator to offer its services to viewers. As a result, city governments around the United States contract with one cable operator to offer services to residents.

To select a cable company, most city governments solicit competitive proposals and, eventually, negotiate a contract with the company offering the best proposal to provide citywide cable services for a fixed number of years. A cable company's contract with a city typically specifies that one or more channels will be dedicated to the dissemination of public information. These channels are called "access" channels. Cable contracts usually stipulate that cable operators will provide funds (often based on a percentage of income from cable services) for the management of these access channels and the production of programming for them.

The number of public access channels varies from city to city, ranging from none to eight or more. A large city typically has about three: a *government access* channel for broadcasting city government hearings or other municipal programs; *an education access* channel for programs, including courses, produced by schools or colleges; and a *public access* channel for broadcasting noncommercial programs produced by citizens and nonprofit organizations. Sometimes these access channels are managed by an independent nonprofit corporation with its own board of directors. Or they could be run by the cable company itself, the city government, a library, or other institutions. Access channels are often managed from community media centers, which might house a variety of other media resources for citizens.

Submit Public Service Announcements

Most access stations—public or government—produce a "Community Bulletin Board" listing nonprofit services and events. The bulletin board is sometimes broadcast for many hours during the day or at night. Commercial notices are not accepted.

"People will give me huge, long announcements that I have to pare down," says Donna Svoboda at City Eight Productions in Dearborn Heights, Michigan, advising citizens to submit announcements of fewer than forty words. "I'm not sure what's the essential information."

Many access channels have forms available for submissions to their bulletin boards. Call to obtain the proper forms.

Broadcast Independently Produced Programs

Most public access stations will broadcast—for free—programs produced by nonprofits or citizen activists. Any member of the community can submit professionally produced pieces.

Staff at the access channels say they prefer videos that have a local focus, but programs with a national perspective are often accepted as well. "We've had them from all over the country," said Connie Mcdonald, administrative coordinator for Bellerica Access Television in Bellerica, Massachusetts. "We have a big recycling group here that's always sending them in." Shorter programs about national subjects (up to 10 minutes) are more readily accepted than longer ones (up to an hour or more). And any national piece is more likely to be aired if submitted by a local group. A public access channel might use the audio portion of a program with a national focus and dub in video with a local angle.

Most public access channels do not allow commercial advertising or monetary solicitations. For example, a church may be able to air a program with religious content, but it could not ask for donations. This rule, like other generalizations about access channels, may vary from city to city.

Many *public* access channels will air controversial programming, but *government* access channels may avoid any controversy. For example, Svoboda at City Eight Productions, whose access channel is managed by the city government, recently rejected an anti-vivisection public service announcement because it was too controversial.

Produce Your Own Program

You can also learn how to operate camera equipment, edit film, and produce your own show for your local public access station. Most offer classes, equipment, and a time slot for your program, depending on availability. This training probably won't run more than $50 and could cost you nothing.

"If a nonprofit gives us a couple of staff, we'll train them," says Earnest at Community Access Television of Salina. "They can come in and create their own program. We try to make it as easy as possible—so anyone can do it."

Most public access channels give citizens total editorial control of programs they produce. This is the dream of many activists tired of squeezing two sentences into the local TV news.

Unfortunately, producing video is time consuming, especially for busy nonprofit staff. A regular program, in particular, can chew up large chunks of time. One way to clear this obstacle is to have volunteers—or student interns—do the show. Unpaid nonprofit staff have successfully produced programs on public access television. Another option: Some cable companies will produce a one-time program for nonprofits at minimal cost. Once produced, this program can be aired repeatedly on the cable access channel.

Who Watches Cable Access?

The major downside of using cable access is that relatively few people tune to it—even though about a third of U.S. citizens subscribe to cable television. One reason: The access channels are usually in the fifties on the TV dial (e.g., channel 54), well away from the zone of most channel surfers. Also, the quality of programming—precisely because much of it is produced by citizens and nonprofit organizations—is usually spotty. In addition, most of the access programming isn't publicized or even listed in TV schedules. Many access channels have no programming (literally a static-filled screen) for much of the day.

If your target audience is watching cable access, you should consider using it. Joan Burke, executive director of the Community Access Center in Kalamazoo, Michigan, says people interested in local government watch cable access in her area. Others say seniors watch. Try to find out from staff at your local access channel who tunes in in your area. You might have to take a plunge and see what happens. The animal shelter in Michigan that doubled its adoption rate for dogs after it began its *Doggy in the Window* program probably had no idea the show would be successful. You may be surprised by how many people will see your item on cable access as they sit mesmerized on their couches, surfing with the remote channel selector for the show that will brighten their evening. On one cable access show, I called Hank Brown, then a senator from Colorado, a "bum" for not endorsing an immediate halt to nuclear weapons testing. Greenpeace got significantly more response from that one comment than it does from the usual "reaction" quote buried at the end of an article about the latest environmental disaster.

As channels on cable television become increasingly valuable, more pressure will be applied by cable companies to cut back on the number of access channels they are required to offer to their subscribers. Already, commercial entertainment channels are beginning to squeeze out not only access channels but commercial news and information channels as well. In the long run, television broadcast via satellite may render cable obsolete. But for now, as long as municipal governments insist that contracts with cable companies include guarantees that access channels will be provided and funds made available for programming, most cable television will continue to offer unusual opportunities for nonprofits to publicize their causes.

27

Use Community Calendars and Public Service Announcements

FIND OUT WHICH news organizations—print and broadcast—in your media market have calendars listing community events and become familiar with them. You'll discover that newspapers have the widest selection, often featuring distinct listings for entertainment, business, sports, religion, and more. Alternative weeklies would not be alternative weeklies without calendar listings.

Calendar editors want to hear from you. Getting your information is their job.

Mail a truncated press release to calendar editors, clearly stating the essential information about your event: who, what, where, when, and a contact name and phone number. (See Chapter 9, "Write a News Release.")

"Just yesterday, I was looking at a wonderful poster about an event, but it didn't have any location or time on it," says Kim Tondryk, editorial assistant at the *Milwaukee Journal Sentinel.* "That's the information I need."

Also send art or photos that can be used to illustrate your event. Community groups don't send in enough quality photos or illustrations to calendar editors. Find out if your photo requires a signed release form. Sometimes calendar editors have to

183

Planned Parenthood®
of the Rocky Mountains

Calendar Listing
Contact: Lisa Shiroff
(303) 832-5991

September 10, 1995

Panel Discussion: Talking With Teens About SEX
for Parents & Educators
Hosted by Planned Parenthood October 24

October is National Family Sexuality Education Month. In recognition of this occasion, Planned Parenthood is hosting a Panel Discussion for parents and educators to help them with the sensitive and difficult topic of sex and sexuality. Even the most eloquent speakers get tongue-tied when it's time to have "The Talk" with their own children!

WHAT: Panel Discussion: Talking with Teens About SEX

WHO: For parents, counselors, educators and youth group leaders

WHEN: Tuesday, October 24, 1995
          6:30 p.m. to 8:30 p.m.

WHERE: Planned Parenthood Educational Resource Center
          919 E. 14th Avenue, Capitol Hill, Denver

RSVP: 832-5991

This event is free and open to the public.
Light refreshments will be provided.

950 Broadway, Denver, Colorado 80203-2779 • 303-321-PLAN • FAX 303-861-0268 • Clinic Appointment 1-800-230-PLAN • Facts of Life Line (303) 832-5995

A calendar item listing all the essential information about the event. Credit: Planned Parenthood of the Rocky Mountains

"scrounge" for art or photos. You never know if your photo—even if you think it's weak—will be needed.

Tips for Getting Listed
in Community Calendars

- Get your information in on time. You should send most releases at least two weeks in advance, but earlier is better. Different calendars in the same paper have different deadlines—one for a music magazine, another for a Sunday events calendar, and yet another for the religion section. Call calendar editors to find out about deadlines and special needs—or check the written policy in the newspaper.
- Double check your information. Calendar editors are brimming with stories about wrong dates, phone numbers, and so on.
- Mail your information. Some outlets prohibit faxing and e-mailing calendar material.
- Don't phone in your item. "We don't take anything over the phone because of the volume I get on a weekly basis," says Kim Tondryk at the *Milwaukee Journal Sentinel*. (She gets 400 to 600 pieces of mail per week.)
- Some editors advise *not* calling to make sure they received your information, but you should call anyway. Over time you will know whom you don't need to bother with a follow-up call.
- Don't forget that your local cable-access station probably has a listing of upcoming events.
- Ask if color photos are accepted.

Public Service Announcements (PSAs)

Broadcast outlets air information about events. Even commercial television stations run video PSAs—albeit often in the middle of the night. The tips for placing calendar items also apply to PSAs, and remember:

At radio stations, call the DJs directly and ask them to read your announcement on the air. Call DJs at any radio station on each shift—even if they don't normally read the news. This works. I've convinced dozens of DJs to plug rallies and events.

Hold a press conference if a PSA is rejected because it's "too controversial" or "not in the public interest." This turns your PSA into news, which might appear on the TV news or in the news section of the paper. You'll reach far more people this way than you ever would if your PSA had been accepted. (See Chapter 4, "Create Newsworthy Visual Imagery, Symbols, and Stunts.")

Some radio stations request that you submit information on a three-by-five-inch card.

28

Shine the Media Spotlight on Nonprofit Products

NONPROFITS OFTEN SELL PRODUCTS to support their cause—even if they're ridiculous ones like Planned Parenthood's underwear printed with condoms. Any nonprofit organization with a product for sale can learn a lot by observing how for-profit businesses market their products.

I like reading business books about marketing, especially because the tomes about marketing for nonprofits are so boring you have to plunge yourself in a bath of ice water every half-hour to stay awake while reading them. Bookstores have large sections of lively business marketing books waiting for you to skim, if not buy and study. Most are written for small businesses, which—like many activists—are scrambling for media attention.

The sections of these business marketing books explaining how to use the news media cover some of what I've laid out in this "cause-oriented" book—how to write press releases, when to distribute them, and so on. But the business books also discuss at length how to present a "product" to the media in a newsworthy way. If you read these books and scrutinize media coverage of products and businesses, you'll discover there are three broad reasons products become news (not including the usual business and crisis coverage of goods, such as the story of contaminated Perrier).

Link the Product to the Public Interest

Nonprofits don't usually have to worry about making a special point to cast what they do as being good for the public. Their activities, by IRS definition, serve the public. But when you are trying to convince a journalist to do a story about your nonprofit product, you should ask yourself how it contributes to the public good. Does it benefit public safety or health? Does it save money or time? Can it be used for a holiday gift? How does it address a current political issue? Can you connect it to breaking news?

For example, recently I was trying to generate news stories about the book *Venus Revealed* by David Harry Grinspoon. It turns out there were numerous ways to link the book to the social issues raised by the questions just given. Public safety? *Venus Revealed* discusses clues to averting global warming. Money or time? *Venus Revealed* critiques congressional spending on space programs. A holiday gift? Full of funky references to pop culture, *Venus Revealed* was published right around Valentine's Day. A current political issue? Again, *Venus Revealed* argues for more money for the embattled space program. A connection to breaking news? *Venus Revealed* theorizes that life could exist on Venus, and it arrived in bookstores just after news was released that scientists had discovered evidence that life may have existed on Mars.

In the end, the author and I chose the book's links to Valentine's Day and life in the solar system. We scheduled a book signing a few days before Valentine's Day (to inspire feature stories) and pitched the life-on-Venus theory to science writers at newspapers to generate news stories. Both worked to some extent. The life-on-Venus theory proved particularly good fodder for talk radio.

Do Something for the Public Good

If their products are either too ordinary or inextricably greed-related, businesspeople break into the news by doing a "good work" that has nothing to do with their businesses. Or, alternatively, they make news by doing something fun that also has nothing to do with their businesses. Nonprofits can expand the visibility of their causes and their products in this way too. Here are some options:

Dedicate part or all of the money from the product to a specific community project like the establishment of a sexual-harassment hotline.

Offer free samples of your product or discounts on it.

Invite a celebrity, for example, a professional athlete, to endorse your product and have a reception.

Organize a cleanup campaign of some kind (for example, a river cleanup).

Offer a free class related to the product. (I teach a course called "Let the World Know: Make Your Cause News.")

Sponsor something outrageous. (A microbrewery sponsors a running-of-the-pigs day downtown. It doesn't matter that pigs have nothing to do with beer as long as the pigs are, in fact, running around!)

Sponsor a contest.

Spot Trends and Be Opportunistic

Here are some ideas for capturing some of the media attention heaped on trendy topics:

Remember that the media are always looking for stories about anything related to holidays and seasons, including products.

Provide expert information linked to breaking news—and ask that you be identified as the inventor or producer of your product.

Consider whether your product relates to a local or national anniversary.

Your product may have a niche in the latest craze.

Link your product to a major event planned for your city. (For example, during the 1996 Republican national convention, an ice cream store in San Diego captured national media attention by naming flavors of ice cream after the Republican presidential candidates.)

29

Publicize a Report
or Academic Paper

THIS CHAPTER IS FOR ACADEMICS who write papers and reports *and* nonprofit groups or activists who do the same. Open any newspaper and you'll see how the news media feed on quantifiable information and new research data (e.g., "An article in *Science* magazine, published today, reveals that . . ."). Statistics on almost any topic of interest can be big newsmakers: crime rates, consumer patterns, sales, polls, and so forth. Soon-to-be-published findings from journals are a major news source.

Nonprofit organizations take advantage of information-hungry reporters by releasing reports and polls of their own. For example, the Center for Science in the Public Interest draws lots of media attention for its studies of the fat content of Chinese food, diet foods, and other comestibles. Data about almost any concern—from the environment to homelessness—can be news.

To the chagrin of serious scientists, journalists sometimes cover pseudoscientific reports—based on humorous or quirky anecdotal information—with the same gusto as they do reports based on years of careful research. For example, depending on the timing of the release of the report, a one-day poll of ten high school classes showing that only 10 percent can identify the first sentence of the Bill of Rights might get as much ink as a ten-year analysis of the causes of illiteracy.

In any case, the fact remains that reports with quantifiable information are attractive to journalists. The key is to simplify and explain the information so that it meets their needs. Also, like most people in our TV culture, broadcast journalists want images to accompany data. Your report with powerful statistics may be covered in every newspaper in the country, but without an image that can carry it to the tube, the effect on many people will be muted. Numbers crack open the back door to the news, but images can shove the front door wide open.

News-induced Headaches and Tips on How to Avoid Them

Many careful researchers and writers are frustrated by the news and choose to avoid journalists altogether. Journalism can fall short of the exacting standards set by detail-oriented people for the following reasons:

- News seldom offers more than two opposing opinions even though most issues have many sides to consider. Unfortunately, journalists lack space for more information, and many don't seek other views because their job is widely considered done when two sides are captured.
- Journalists value simple information, whereas reality is complex. As a result, some stories are completely shut out of the news, especially television news, and others are simplified to the point of being meaningless. "There are important stories that don't fit into the two-minute format," says Peter Dykstra, a senior producer for Cable News Network.
- Journalists downplay uncertainty, especially in headlines. Just the presence of an article in a newspaper—regardless of what it says—implies certainty.
- Between deadline pressures and staff cuts, the facts inevitably get twisted sometimes despite the best efforts of journalists.

- Science is overshadowed by personalities and politics. The substance of many debates in the news takes a backseat to who's winning and what that person is doing.
- Crisis coverage is emphasized. This means that many important issues are ignored until a crisis occurs. How much coverage do you see of African poverty until starvation strikes or a war starts?
- News is image-based and event-centered. Issues and ideas that don't lend themselves to visual imagery are often shut out of the news.
- Quotations can be distorted. Sound bites are sometimes incapable of expressing truth.

You cannot avoid all of these headaches because many arise out of the nature of journalism. But here are some ways to relieve, if not eliminate, many of them.

- Don't leave it to journalists to simplify your complex information. Recognize journalistic realities and simplify your information for them.
- Know deadlines and give journalists enough time to review your information. Don't force journalists to make mistakes because they are rushing. (See Chapter 5, "Choose a Time to Maximize Coverage.")
- Tell a journalist the name of someone who "opposes" your position. If you supply a reasonable "other side," you lessen the likelihood that a reporter will quote a quack who opposes you.
- Don't overwhelm journalists with information, especially written information. Think about the limited space journalists work with and decide precisely what slice of your information you want them to use. (See the next section.)
- Tell journalists directly, perhaps at the end of an interview, what you think is the most important aspect of your report.

- Accept the event-centered nature of news and turn the release of your report into an event, using an appropriate visual. For example, if your report is about frogs, make some frogs available for photographers at a news conference. Highlight the planned appearance of the frogs in your news release.
- Take advantage of "crisis coverage" by releasing your information when the media is focusing on a crisis related to your expertise. If there's an oil spill and you've got data showing that routine oil leaks are a more serious threat than large spills, release your data when coverage is focusing on the crisis.
- Don't take journalism too seriously. A mistake or a distortion in the news media isn't that big a deal (though in some cases internal politics at a university or elsewhere demand caution). Just keep trying to get the word out. It's the cumulative efforts that count.

If you are willing to accept some of the hazards and limitations of journalism and want to publicize your report in the news media, note that the nuts and bolts for attracting media attention to a report are similar to those for drawing the media to an event. Thus even if you have no interest in staging an event or stunt around your report, flip through Part 1 of this book, paying close attention to the chapters cited in the following steps on planning your strategy:

Step 1.   Determine your goal. As with all media outreach, decide what you're trying to accomplish. Why do you want media attention? Do you want to affect legislation? Educate the public?

Step 2.   Who's your audience? Do you want your information to be seen by policymakers? The general public? A swing vote in the legislature? A regional audience? Some academics prefer to pass their information to advocates and let them publicize it. In this case, outreach—not media coverage—is required. Or maybe you want to target advocacy media outlets (e.g., environmental magazines published by environmental organizations).

Step 3.   Identify a message and media outlets that will reach your audience. Once you've established who your audience is, you can target media outlets that are appropriate. And you can tailor a message and—if necessary—a visual image to your target audience and media outlets. (See Chapter 1, "Develop a Simple Message.")

Step 4.   Choose a time and location (see Chapter 5, "Choose a Time to Maximize Coverage," and Chapter 6, "Find an Effective Location"), compile a media list (see Chapter 8, "Compile a Media List"), and write a news release (see the following example and Chapter 9, "Write a News Release").

Step 5.   Distribute your news release. Many journalists aren't using e-mail yet, so usually it's best to fax it. However, you may be able to use e-mail effectively to contact reporters covering technical subjects. For example, Jim Scott, public information officer at the University of Colorado at Boulder, has located a list of 450 top astronomy writers. The list is maintained by a press officer at the American Astronomical Society. It would be worth checking around to find out if there's an e-mail list of journalists covering your area of expertise. "Even though we use e-mail, the most important thing is to call these people," says Scott. (Also see Chapter 10, "Distribute a News Release.")

Step 6.   Prepare for interviews and call reporters. Unless you expect major coverage, you do not need to hold a press conference to discuss your report with journalists. It's easier for reporters to speak to you on the phone. If you've got a visual image to accom-

196

Rocky
Mountain
Media Watch

P.O. Box 18858
Denver CO 80218
303 832-7558

FOR IMMEDIATE RELEASE   April 17, 1997

Contact: Jason Salzman
303-433-6961 or 303-832-7558

NATIONAL NEWSPAPER SURVEY REVEALS "PUNDIT GENDER GAP"
New York Times Tops List With Only 17% of Op-Eds Written by Women

At a time when women are making significant steps toward equality in the business world, 75% of opinion columns on the commentary pages of U.S. newspapers are authored by men, according to a study released today by Rocky Mountain Media Watch.

The study, which analyzed all op-eds appearing in seven newspapers during September, 1996, reveals:

- Nationally, 75% of op-eds are written by men. At the *New York Times*, 83% of op-eds are written by men. The *Los Angeles Times* follows a close second at 81%. Next is the *Washington Post* at 78%, followed by the *Chicago Tribune* (72%), *Denver Post* (72%), *USA Today* (72%), and *Rocky Mountain News* (65%).

- The survey also noted the number of op-eds written by guests unaffiliated with the newspaper. (These are writers who are not staff, syndicated, or regular freelancers.) The three local papers in the survey print few columns by guest writers. Eleven percent of op-eds in the *Denver Post* (down from 18% in 1995), 7% of op-eds in the *Rocky Mountain News* (same as 1995), and 21% of op-eds in the *Chicago Tribune* were written by guests.

- Former or current government officials authored the most op-eds in the *New York Times* and *USA Today*. Representatives of citizen advocacy groups were given the least op-ed space in the *Chicago Tribune, Los Angeles Times, New York Times,* and *Washington Post.*

Rocky Mountain Media Watch is a Denver-based non-profit organization founded in 1994 to challenge the news media, particularly local TV news, to resist tabloid coverage and air stories that inform and connect our communities. Its publications, including "Pavlov's TV Dogs: A Snapshot of Local TV News in America," "Baad News," and *Let the World Know: Make Your Cause News,* have received national acclaim.

-- 30 --

A press release highlighting the major findings of a report in simple language. Credit: Rocky Mountain Media Watch pany your report, you will need some sort of media event even if it's just a news conference. (See Chapter 11, "Become a Master Interviewee," and Chapter 12, "Call a Reporter After You've Sent a News Release.")

Tips for Making a Report More Newsworthy

- Develop a short (three to ten pages), faxable executive summary. Make the full report available upon request.
- Upload your executive summary and full report to a Web site on the Internet and list the site's address on your news release. "It's a good way to make information available rather than faxing an entire report," says Tom Lippman, a diplomatic correspondent for the *Washington Post*.
- In a news release, emphasize just a few statistics. Remember, most news stories don't cover many points.
- Use clear, attractive graphs or tables and short paragraphs without jargon.
- Connect your report to a news peg. (See Chapter 5, "Choose a Time to Maximize Coverage.")
- If possible, show a change in data from the previous year.
- Create quirky titles for trends or other data (e.g., "gender gap").
- If you are affiliated with an academic institution, take advantage of the public relations office at most universities for media contacts and other help. Print your news release on university letterhead. Include your title.
- Make numbers more meaningful by using comparisons or breaking them down into units that are more comprehensible (e.g., *Media Advocacy and Public Health* cites figures indicating that the alcohol industry spends $2 billion annually on advertising—$225,000 for every hour of the day).
- Localize news releases about a national report and send them directly to local journalists. (An Environmental De-

fense Fund report showed that most U.S. endangered
species could be saved if key areas in the U.S. were protected. It crafted news releases for media outlets near
those key areas.)
• In addition to releasing your report to the news media,
consider publishing a short summary of it as a guest opinion in the newspaper. (See Chapter 20, "Write a Guest
Opinion.")

30

Promote a Story
to Journalists at
National News Outlets

JOURNALISTS AT NATIONAL NEWS OUTLETS are busier and harder to reach than their local counterparts. Otherwise, the keys to promoting a story at the national level are largely the same as promoting a story at the local level. This holds true whether you're trying to access news reporters, talk-radio producers, TV talk-show producers, TV "news magazine" producers, newspaper columnists, feature writers, editorial page editors, or any journalist at a national outlet. (You can also convince photo editors at national news magazines to buy photos of events. This is easier if you hire a professional "freelance" photographer to shoot photos for you. Photos taken by your organization aren't as easily sold to photo editors.) Most of the same techniques apply: Keep it simple, know deadlines, be professional, contact the right person, have the proper written information, use contacts, and study the tips in this book.

If you live in a major metropolitan area, a national news outlet might have a bureau with full-time staff in your city. For example, CBS News maintains a bureau in Miami. NBC News has one in Chicago.

If you don't live in a major city, contact "stringers," local representatives of national media outlets, if there are any in your area. This is more effective than trying to reach a journalist on the phone at the outlet's national headquarters in New York, Washington, D.C., or another large city. (If you live in a city where the national outlet is headquartered, you should call journalists at the main office.) A stringer for a national news outlet often works on the staff of a local outlet. For example, when I lived in Providence, Rhode Island, I pitched my stories for the *New York Times* to its Providence stringer, who worked at the *Providence Journal*. From Denver, I pitched stories for National Public Radio to its staffer in Salt Lake City or to its local stringer at KGNU radio in Boulder.

If a national news outlet doesn't have a bureau or stringers in your city, you'll have to call its regional bureau or headquarters. (To find out whether there are bureaus in your area, call the outlet's headquarters or check the yellow pages of the phone book and books listing national news media in the library. For stringers, ask people familiar with your local media market.)

The keys to making national news are having a story that merits national attention and being persistent. "Particularly for *Newsweek*, the threshold is higher," says Michael Hirsh, a Washington, D.C., correspondent for *Newsweek*. "It's got to illustrate a trend as opposed to a tidbit."

"We only have 22 minutes of news," says Tom Donahue, Miami bureau chief for CBS News. "That isn't much, especially after we do Washington news and stuff like that."

You'll be amazed at how the national media follow each other. Once your story is covered by one outlet, others will come. "I can pitch a story here [to other journalists at CNN] until I'm blue in the face—until it appears in the *New York Times*," says Peter Dykstra, a senior producer at Cable News Network. "Then the response is, 'Why haven't you been on top of this?'" Tomi Ervamaa, a Washington, D.C.–based correspondent for *Helsingin Sanomat*, a major paper in Finland, says, "We steal ideas from each other. I read the *New York Times* and *Washington Post* to get ideas."

Associated Press Is
a Gateway to National Coverage

News outlets from around the country "subscribe" to news services, which—in return—transmit news stories, photos, video, and other information to their subscribers. The subscribers can use information from news services in their broadcasts or publications. The quantity and type of information that news outlets receive from news services vary according to the type of subscription they buy. For example, a news service might have a menu of news available, including sports, weather, business, and statewide, national, and international news.

The largest news service in the United States is the Associated Press (AP). For most nonprofit organizations, small and large, the Associated Press is the gateway to national media attention. The most likely way that your story will be distributed beyond your city—either regionally or nationally—is via the AP.

The AP is a not-for-profit corporation owned by the news outlets that subscribe to it. A news outlet signs a contract with AP stipulating that it and AP exchange news with each other and that the news outlet may broadcast AP's news stories and AP may distribute its subscribers' news to other subscribers around the world.

AP does not cover many local stories with its own reporters, taking them instead from newspapers. "The San Francisco bureau does not cover the city of San Francisco," says Bill Schiffmann, a news editor for AP's San Francisco bureau. "We let local papers cover it. If it's something of state-wide interest, we'll take it out of the paper the next morning. We only cover stories that are of interest nationally."

Even when AP does assign a reporter to cover a local story, local newspapers tend *not* to use AP coverage, preferring stories written by their own staffs. But they often rely heavily on AP for news about national or international topics. Thus your story on the AP wire may be used in every newspaper across the country *except* your local one. In contrast, local broadcast media, especially radio stations without news reporters on staff, rely on AP reports for both local and national news. Many radio DJs "rip and read," which refers to taking a story from the AP printout and reading it immediately on the air.

The AP in the United States is divided into "bureaus" and "desks." A bureau may be responsible for covering news in one or more states or a large metropolitan area. For example, the San Francisco bureau has twelve staff. Colorado and Wyoming are lumped in one bureau with "correspondents" in Cheyenne (four), Grand Junction (one), and Denver (ten). Colorado news media that subscribe to AP generally receive at least the stories about Colorado and Wyoming from the Colorado-Wyoming bureau, which may transmit fifty to sixty pieces per day on the wire, plus about six photos. Some news outlets, such as regional newspapers, subscribe to other states' AP wires.

If the Colorado-Wyoming, San Francisco, or any other AP bureau believes that one of its stories is of national interest, it forwards the story to the national news "desk" in New York. Editors there decide whether it's placed on the national wire—to be sent to AP subscribers around the country. "We send them things that we think are of national interest," says Schiffmann at AP in San Francisco.

If a story from a bureau is of international interest, it is sent to the foreign desk in New York or Washington, D.C. From there, it could be zapped around the world. There are multiple foreign wires covering different regions of the world. Stories on some of these wires are translated into different languages. (Read more about the Associated Press and other news services in Chapter 8, "Compile a Media List.")

Six Ways to Increase Your Chances of AP Coverage

1. AP is a service that responds to its clients, which are news media outlets that pay a fee to receive AP stories. If you can convince

an AP subscriber to request a photo or story from an AP office, your chances of getting covered are greatly increased. To do this, you need to persuade a reporter, who will not attend your event, to request that AP cover it. A reporter in another city or state could do this. For example, once a Greenpeace colleague convinced a reporter in South Carolina to request an AP photo of a protest in Denver. Sure enough, an AP photographer attended our protest and a photo was distributed nationally.

2. AP often runs stories on its national wire that affect many states. For example, rankings of states according to various comparatives such as "most livable" or "most affluent" are widely distributed by AP. If you are promoting a story with this kind of wide appeal, you should make an extra effort to convince AP to cover you.

3. Use your contacts. A colleague knew a professor who was a former national editor at AP. We were having problems convincing AP to cover a report, and we called the professor for ideas. He gave us the name of someone in the New York AP office, whom we contacted. The next week our story was distributed nationally by AP. (You should be wary of pitching a story to any AP office other than the one in your area—unless your story relates to a national issue that is normally covered in Washington, D.C.)

4. Sometimes AP will buy photos of your event if an AP photographer didn't make it to the event. If you've got a good story, bring your photos to the AP office. A freelance photographer's work is best, but it's not required. (You can also bring your dramatic home video to television stations if they did not show up. See Chapter 14, "Alert the Media to Surprise Events and Civil Disobedience.")

5. Contact AP photographers directly by fax and phone. They can make independent decisions on whether an event merits a photograph, which may be distributed to media outlets around the world. "The photo decision is often made separate from the news decision," says David Briscoe at the Associated Press.

"Maybe a demonstration is taking place about a routine issue [that doesn't merit a news story], but it's visually interesting." (You can also talk to photo editors at AP about taking your own photos at your event and bringing the undeveloped film to them immediately after the event takes place.)

6. Associated Press reporters like to have a news story a little before other news outlets get it so that the story can be distributed before it's officially released. To accommodate AP, you might, for example, give AP your story a day or two before you release it at a news conference on February 17 at 10 A.M. EST. If you have embargoed your story for 8 A.M. EST on the day of your conference, then AP would—you hope—put your story on the wire around 8 A.M. and possibly update it at your 10 A.M. news conference. Prior notice also gives AP the opportunity to schedule a time slot for the story to be distributed electronically.

One Example of How a Local Story Can Become National News

In fall 1996, the U.S. Postal Service announced plans to abandon its historic building in downtown Livingston, Montana, and build a new facility on the edge of town. Local residents objected to the relocation, arguing that a "Wal-Mart style" post office was not appropriate for their town. A group of citizens immediately organized to spearhead the fight to keep the post office in the existing building, which was listed on the National Register of Historic Places.

The group organized support in town and, with a series of press releases, elevated the issue to the front page of several local papers. The story quickly became statewide news in Montana.

Next, the activists identified Montana-based stringers for national publications. They called the journalists and pitched the post office story to them. Not all the national journalists jumped at the story, but bit by bit, interest began to grow, especially after the *New York Times* ran an article about it. *Time* magazine followed, publishing a full-page piece about the campaign titled "It Breaks a Village."

It turned out that citizens in other small U.S. towns were facing the same problem: The post office was abandoning old buildings in favor of large, new facilities. So the Montana story was emblematic of a national trend. This helped convince reporters that the story was worthy of a national audience. Soon pieces about the Livingston post office appeared in the *Washington Post* and the *Christian Science Monitor* and on National Public Radio.

"When the story started appearing in East Coast papers, the postmaster general got upset," says activist Dennis Glick. That's when the tide turned, and the post office announced that it would renovate its downtown Livingston office and build a smaller processing facility out of town. The activists won even though the fight looked impossible at the outset.

"We tend to look at insurmountable odds as a problem," says Glick, adding that his group was careful to paint the postal service in Washington, D.C., as the bad guys, not the local workers in Livingston. "But it actually worked in our favor. When you portray yourself as David versus Goliath, the press love it. And, in fact, that was the exact situation we found ourselves in. But instead of stones and a slingshot, we used press releases and a fax machine."

Glick says the media campaign was key to their success. "Toward the end, the *Today* show called," he says. "It's funny how this stuff snowballs. Once you get some coverage, it all starts rolling in."

31

Generate
News Coverage Abroad

IF YOU'RE PROTESTING the importation of grapes laced with dangerous pesticide residues, your campaign would probably benefit from news coverage in countries that export grapes. To get news coverage abroad, don't rely on U.S. news outlets or services to transmit your story around the world even though some—for example, the Associated Press—have the capability to do this. Contact news media from foreign countries directly.

It turns out that if your story is appropriate, getting international media coverage is not too difficult. In fact, sometimes you'll be able to get more media attention abroad than you'll receive in this country.

Some publicists know this and use it to pressure foreign countries. For example, in the mid-1980s, the New Zealand government banned all U.S. nuclear-powered and nuclear-armed warships from docking in its ports. The Kiwis figured that bringing nuclear bombs to the South Pacific was an example of the Cold War run amok. But the Reagan administration and its allies in Congress didn't see it that way. To punish New Zealand, the administration eventually withdrew the United States from all treaty obligations to come to the aid of its longtime ally down under.

Leading up to the decision to abandon New Zealand, anti–New Zealand forces in Washington stepped up public pressure on the New Zealanders. They knew that the nuclear issue was so sensitive in the United States that any development here would be big news there.

One of the ways they generated huge headlines in New Zealand was to introduce a bill in Congress attacking the country, which has about 4 million people and 60 million sheep. The introduction of a bill in the U.S. Congress is a nonevent. It means practically nothing because so many bills are introduced and virtually none pass. In fact, only a small percentage of bills introduced in Congress are even brought to a vote. (Many are introduced by one crusading member of the House of Representatives who has lined up no co-sponsors for the proposed legislation.) The two-page New Zealand bill introduced in the House called for, among other things, banning all lamb imports from New Zealand! You can imagine the headlines in the Kiwi press. Here, of course, there was only minimal coverage, and there was never a vote on the bill.

A response in the United States—even if it's by a small activist group—to a sensitive issue in a foreign country is usually news there. "If there's a Dutch angle, I will go for it," says Oscar Garchagen, a reporter for *Devolkskrant*, a major paper in the Netherlands. But he emphasizes that his job is to cover what's happening in the United States, not to focus on issues related to the Netherlands. "NGOs [non-governmental organizations] are very effective, available, and very helpful," he says. "I use NGOs as a source just as I use government sources."

U.S.-based foreign correspondents are not hard to reach. (See the tips in this chapter.) But like other journalists, they face time constraints and deadline pressures. Often, one reporter has the staggering job of covering the entire United States, including major political events. These reporters should be approached as you would any other busy journalist.

"I do stories about people," says reporter Tomi Ervamaa, a Washington, D.C., reporter for *Helsingin Sanomat*, a large newspaper in Finland. "I try to get out of D.C. and do feature stories about life in the U.S."

Tips for Obtaining Lists of Foreign Journalists

- For a list of news media in a specific country, call the embassy or consulate of that country and ask for it. You can request names of foreign journalists working in the United States as well as in their own country. This does not produce results all the time, but it's worth a try.
- Check international media directories. Bacon's publishes one, but your local library may have others that will work. These directories should list foreign media with U.S. offices. The U.S. State Department also publishes a list of foreign media. (See Chapter 39, "Sources for Lists of News Outlets.")
- Many large foreign media outlets maintain offices in Washington, D.C., and many are located in the National Press Club on 14th Street, which distributes a list of building occupants.
- Some countries have their own national news services (such as Japan's Jiji Press, Agence France-Presse in France, Yonhap for South Korea, and Xinhau for China), which might be interested in your story and have representatives in the United States. Reuters is Europe's major news service. Focus on these first, as they will distribute your story widely. (For more information on news services, see Chapter 8, "Compile a Media List.")
- Contact an allied group that promotes stories internationally. As always, it's best not to have to reinvent the media list.
- It's easier to pitch your story to foreign journalists based in the United States—probably in New York, Washington, D.C., or San Francisco—than to journalists abroad. These reporters may not attend your news conference in Austin,

Texas, but they might take your story over the phone. They also might be interested in obtaining photos from you. If you're serious and have the proper language skills, you can call abroad or e-mail.

Tips for Attracting
Foreign Journalists to a Story

- As described previously, even the most trivial actions by the U.S. Congress can make big news abroad. It's worth the effort to pressure a member of Congress to act—introduce a bill, sponsor a resolution, or even simply write a letter.
- Issue a "reaction" news release containing your quote related to breaking news about a foreign country. Quotes praising foreign countries are often picked up, too. (See "Tips for Reacting to Breaking News" in Chapter 17, "Suggest Ideas for News Stories to Journalists.")
- Have someone from a foreign country "do something" here in the United States (e.g., write a report, participate in an event) and feature the foreigner in your press materials—with any other information you want to promote.
- Find out if a U.S. company has foreign partners. If so, you can promote your event related to the U.S. company not only to the U.S. media but also to the media of the country of its partners.
- Bring your own photographers to a meeting with foreign officials and distribute the video or photographs of the meeting to the foreign press with the story.
- Organize a coalition of nonprofit groups or notables (e.g., political figures, business leaders, celebrities) to send a joint letter to a foreign government and announce it in a press release. Such letters would receive little or no coverage in the United States but could be news abroad.

- Hold an event (protest, delivery, stunt) at a company, consulate, or embassy of a foreign country. Even a few protesters can make news. For example, Greenpeace organized a rally of about forty people in front of the Taiwan trade mission to protest shipments of nuclear waste from Taiwan to North Korea. The media efforts, which yielded major coverage, focused on China, Taiwan, and Korea. "Even just a few protesters can make news abroad," says Tom Clements of Greenpeace International. "We've had great success getting in the foreign media, even with simple protests in the U.S."

Tips for Generating News at an International Summit

Often thousands of journalists from around the world converge on a city to cover a summit or meeting of international leaders. This is an opportunity—although a difficult one—to capture the attention of the world's media.

- Get media credentials. This allows you access to the media headquarters, where you can pitch your story directly to journalists. To get credentials, you may have to apply a month or so in advance. Check for a Web site of the international summit you want to attend and look for information on media credentials.
- Find a list of attending journalists. Call the local press office that's set up for the international meeting. Also, stop by the desk where journalists pick up their press credentials and ask for a comprehensive list of journalists who've been granted credentials.
- Identify the hotels where the foreign journalists are staying and deliver news releases there. You can also fax news releases to hotel guests.

- Determine where, in the media headquarters, journalists from various countries have their assigned work stations and deliver news releases to targeted countries.
- Explain in news releases why your story or event would be of particular interest to journalists from specific countries.
- Create a visual image that can be easily accessed by photographers. Often, meetings of international leaders are slim on visuals, so yours could make a hit. Highlight the visual aspect of your event in your news release or flyer, which should be circulated inside media headquarters. Stage your event as close to headquarters as possible.
- Pitch your story directly to journalists whenever possible. Convincing individual journalists of the merits of your story is probably the most effective way to get coverage.
- Use personal contacts. If you know journalists—or if you think specific publications will cover your issue—try them first.
- Hold a local media event or stunt the day before the summit starts. This will put your issue in the local newspaper as foreign journalists arrive in town.

Part Three

How to Handle Unsolicited Media Attention

Sometimes the tables are turned and journalists call on you without being beckoned. This attention can simply be a sign that your media work is effective: Journalists are turning to you for information. Despite any misgivings you might have, you're considered an expert—or your organization has been recognized as legitimate.

Sometimes you'd rather journalists go away. Part 3 provides information on how to deal responsibly with reporters when your organization faces a crisis that attracts them. It also outlines a process for you to handle routine—but unsolicited—calls from journalists who seek comments, data, or any other kind of information.

32

Control a Media Crisis

ANY NONPROFIT ORGANIZATION can face a disaster: Your delivery truck hits a pedestrian. Your opponents sue you, claiming defamation. One of your dinners for senior citizens is laced with poison. A sexual assault is reported in your building. Even if you think your organization is benign and powerless, serious problems can arise, placing you in the harsh light of the media.

The general rule in these circumstances is to release as much information as you can as soon as you can. This fosters a better working relationship between you and the media—and ultimately citizens. But release only information that you're absolutely sure is accurate. And make sure your release of information is legal and responsible.

"For us, the more open a group can be, the better," says Cathy Lawhon, team leader for the *Orange County Register*'s Lake Forest bureau. "Usually [groups] tend to circle the wagons and not give information at all. . . . If it's something that's sensitive, it seems to me that they'd be better off coming out with it and telling us their side of the story. We usually get the information anyway."

Prepare a Crisis Communications Plan

Even small nonprofits should develop a plan for dealing with the media in a crisis situation. At a minimum this plan should list a series of tasks to be completed when a crisis strikes (e.g., who

215

should be contacted, documents that should be prepared, specific issues that should be addressed). Then, when a crisis comes, they're far less likely to forget something.

At the heart of the crisis communications plans of many large nonprofits is a crisis communications team, consisting of—among others—the director of the organization, legal counsel, and the directors of public affairs and media relations. When a major crisis arises, these team members can think through the problem together and develop the proper response. At small nonprofits, unfortunately, the crisis communications team may consist of one person who performs multiple jobs—perhaps with consultation available over the phone. But in either case what's important is to make sure that all angles on the crisis are considered.

"Initially, there is quite often a schism between the attorney, who wants to say as little as possible, and the public affairs person, who wants to say as much as possible," says Alex Huppé, director of public affairs for Harvard University. But Huppé says differences can be minimized if staff take time to establish relationships and discuss the issues involved (e.g., legal risks versus public relations) before a crisis arises. Huppé also points out that at larger nonprofits, media crises can be avoided by making sure that all staff know what's a crisis and what isn't.

Tips for Dealing with an Unwanted Media Frenzy

- Answer hypothetical questions with something like, "I don't want to speculate about that. I prefer to wait for the facts."
- Don't estimate or guess. Offer only confirmed, accurate information.
- Release as much information as possible as soon as possible. "Editors and reporters can get information that they think is true and build a story around it that could be far more dam-

aging to the institution than the truth," says Fred Knubel, director of public information for Columbia University.

- Know what information you cannot legally release, and don't feel obliged to divulge all information, including proprietary or personal information.
- Always comment. In fact, as a media spokesperson, you should eliminate the phrase "no comment" from your brain. It makes you sound insensitive, elusive, and guilty. Instead, explain why you can't answer a question. A useful standby answer is, "I am gathering more facts about that issue right now and will respond as soon as possible." Other generic answers are "Our policy is . . . , and I am currently determining if our policy was followed in this case," or "My lawyer has prohibited me from discussing those details."
- Make sure it's clear whom journalists can contact for information, and make sure this person is available around the clock to take media calls.
- Stay calm. Don't get angry. (If you can't control your emotions, appoint a spokesperson who can.)
- The highest-ranking executive available should deliver as many statements to the media as possible in a crisis situation—if he or she is a competent spokesperson. This adds authority, honesty, and sincerity to statements made in a crisis. (That's why all executives should receive interview training.)
- If your nonprofit faces frequent media crises involving government agencies (e.g., the police) or other institutions, establish contacts with personnel at those external agencies.
- Allow plenty of opportunities for journalists to ask questions.
- Don't try to be humorous. It's not worth the risk.
- If you are confronted by reporters unexpectedly, don't walk or run away from the cameras. This footage will almost certainly be used.

Examples of Handling Media in a Crisis

Whether you're associated with a large institution or a tiny organization, your challenge in a crisis situation is to maintain clarity about what information you can legally and responsibly give to journalists while respecting their need for information. Know what you can say and how to get it out.

Did the Unabomber Go to Harvard?

"One afternoon I had about sixty reporters outside my office asking about a fellow named Theodore Kaczynski," says Harvard University's Huppé. "They were asking, 'Did the Unabomber go to Harvard?'"

Huppé understood that he had to respond quickly. But at the same time, he knew he had to respect the privacy of Harvard graduates. First, he pointed out, there was no proof that Theodore Kaczynski was the Unabomber, whether or not the Kaczynski that the FBI had just arrested went to Harvard.

"In fifteen minutes, all I could confirm for sure was that there was a Theodore Kaczynski of the same spelling who graduated from Harvard in the sixties," says Huppé, explaining why he decided against releasing a photo and other information about Kaczynski to journalists. "I had this fear that there was this good old alum named Theodore Kaczynski on a fishing trip who was going to see his photo in the paper and say, 'Wait a minute.' There are a lot of Kaczynskis around and a lot of Theodores."

A Twenty-Million-Gallon Water Leak

"Emergencies always seem to happen at night or over the weekend," says Trina McGuire, media relations manager for Denver Water. "I got one call on the Friday afternoon before Memorial Day. A huge pipe that brought water from the treatment plant to the city had busted." Already, businesses and a major interstate were flooded.

Journalists from all of Denver's major media outlets, who heard about the accident on police scanners, started calling immediately. All McGuire could tell them initially was that she knew the spill had occurred and that the broken pipe was owned by Denver Water.

McGuire made calls to her "crisis team," which includes—among others—key directors and managers from the legal, operations, and public affairs departments. She gathered information as quickly as possible.

"Within fifteen minutes, I called back the journalists and told them the size of the pipe and what it was. I told them it would be a while before we knew why it broke." One news outlet had falsely reported that 200 million gallons were lost when the actual spill was 20 million. She spent the next two hours making sure journalists had the correct information and relaying other information to them as she got it.

"We had relationships [with journalists] in place before this happened," says McGuire, allowing her, if necessary, to say with credibility, "This is wrong." McGuire made sure that she got through to journalists she knew, rather than speaking to interns on the news desk, and that the journalists covering the spill could reach her around the clock.

As the crisis developed, some homes were flooded. "Because we were short staffed, we didn't get to them fast enough," says McGuire. A few news outlets did stories about citizens whose homes were flooded and who were ignored by Denver Water. In response, Denver Water sent a group of employees to offer assistance to flood victims.

Says McGuire: "A bunch of us went door-to-door saying, 'We're from the Water Department. Is everything OK? Is there anything we can do?' We made sure the news media knew about it."

33

Handle an Unsolicited Call from a Journalist

As THE NONPROFIT SECTOR is subject to increased scrutiny by journalists and the public, nonprofit professionals need to be prepared to respond to probing questions even if they do not seek media coverage. You need to know how to deal fairly and effectively with journalists who call. Most often, a journalist's unsolicited call should be taken as a compliment: Your organization is seen as representative of the public and as a source of credible information

Your organization should have a plan to deal with press inquiries even if you choose not to seek them. You don't need a detailed plan, but at a minimum, train one or two people to respond to journalists. Also make sure that your organization's leadership has interviewing skills.

Tips for Responding to an Unsolicited Call from a Journalist

- One or two people in your organization should be designated media liaisons even if you don't have a communications department. Make sure they, at a minimum, read this book. Or better, they should attend a media how-to seminar.
- Make sure everyone who answers the phone knows that calls from journalists should be routed to your designated

media liaison. (This does not mean, however, that others in your organization should be banned from speaking to reporters. Journalists are rightfully skeptical if only a select few are allowed to speak to them. Anyone who wants to speak to reporters should do so—if they are questioned. Of course, this does not mean that everyone should *try* to be interviewed.)

- Always take a reporter's call, but remember you can tell a reporter, once you speak with him or her briefly, that you'll call back.
- When a reporter calls, ask about the interview topic and format (live TV, phone, taped TV, talk radio, visit to the office, etc.).
- If necessary, tell the reporter you'll call back shortly. Remember deadlines. You want to prepare, but you don't want to miss a chance to comment on a story about your organization—even if it's a negative story.
- Make sure the journalist is actually with the news outlet he claims to represent. Call the main number of the outlet and ask if he's on staff.
- Determine who among your executive staff is available for interviews.
- Prepare for interviews. (See Chapter 11, "Become a Master Interviewee.")
- If the reporter wants an immediate interview, quickly run through possible questions and answers with your spokesperson.
- Call the reporter back and work out the logistics of where and when the interview will take place. Or if it is to take place immediately, have your spokesperson call the reporter directly.
- Make a record of all unsolicited calls by reporters. Add names to your media list later.

- Your unsolicited call from a radio or TV journalist could be, essentially, an audition for a show: "If I were working for a TV station, I'd be interviewing you for information *and* auditioning you to see how you'd be on the air," says Peter Dykstra, a senior producer for Cable News Network.

Sample Form for Recording Incoming Calls by Reporters

Media Calls and Response Form

Date Call Received _____

Time Call Received _____

Name of Journalist _____

Title _____

Name or Call Letters of News Outlet _____

Phone _____

Fax _____

E-mail _____

JOURNALIST'S REQUEST:

DEADLINE: _____

Comments:

DATE/TIME REQUEST FILLED: _____

Logged in Media List: _____

Part Four

How to Be a
News Source
and Media Critic

YOU WILL BE MUCH MORE SUCCESSFUL at generating news, as discussed in Parts 1 and 2, if you study the professional etiquette of the journalism world and respect it as you interact with journalists. As a publicist, you have to adjust to the needs and expectations of reporters.

Part 4 outlines how you should act in the universe of reporters. It contains specific suggestions to keep you off the journalistic blacklist and on the lineup of quotable sources. Learn how to become a resource for journalists, develop credibility, and maintain relationships with journalists for the long term. In the following pages, I will also explain when it makes sense to complain about news coverage and how to criticize the news media effectively.

34

Cultivate Relationships
with Journalists

On RARE OCCASIONS, you will stage a single media event and your cause will be won. For example, authorities at a New York mall recently asked a woman who was breastfeeding her newborn to leave. The woman fought back, organizing a dozen women and their babies to breastfeed in unison in the heart of the mall. In the wake of intense media coverage, including national Associated Press photos of the breastfeeders, the New York legislature gave women the explicit right to breastfeed in malls and elsewhere.

This story of inspired—and successful—activism is not the norm. Usually, victory comes after years of work, taking so long that you may not recognize your "victory" when it arrives. As a result, it's essential to develop relationships with journalists that will endure for the long term.

This chapter contains tips on how to establish ongoing relationships with reporters. This is an extremely important aspect of publicizing a cause. You should continually scrutinize how you interact with journalists and strive to improve, sharpening your public relations skills.

"A lot of what gets covered depends on personal relationships at the paper," acknowledges Colin Covert, a feature reporter for the *Star Tribune* in Minneapolis. So, you're thinking, what good does that information do me if I have no such contacts? First, recognize that although helpful, contacts aren't essential. Many journalists will listen to you even if they don't know you. Second, it should inspire you to develop as many contacts as you can.

Say you've just started a new job in a new town, and you want to get to know some journalists. What should you do? "Lunch is too time-consuming," says Jack Broom, a reporter for the *Seattle Times*. "Start with a phone call. Say something like, 'We'd like you to know about us. We've got some events coming up in the next few months. Whom should we contact?'" Starting from there, take advantage of every opportunity to present yourself as a credible source of information for journalists.

Tips on Becoming a Resource for Journalists

- Be available. Each time a reporter calls and can't get through to you, the chances decrease that he or she will call again. But if you earn a reputation for being available, a reporter on a deadline will likely call you instead of someone else for a comment. Give reporters, especially at news services where they work odd hours, your home phone number and tell them it's OK to call.
- Seek out journalists at meetings, hearings, and other events and give them your business card.
- Be ready to be quoted. If a reporter calls for a quote about breaking news and you have to call back before you can comment, you decrease the odds that the reporter will call again. Next time he or she may call someone who does not require the hassle of two phone calls. In fact, you may not be quoted at all because you may not be able to get through to the reporter before deadline. Or he or she may find someone else to comment and file the story before talking to you again.

- Know your issue. Journalists, even those who focus on one issue area, are usually not specialists. They are generalists who get their information from "sources." Your goal should be to become a source. Read and comment intelligently on developments relating to your cause.
- Don't always assume journalists have received information that you have. Call them and ask if they've heard about the upcoming visit of so-and-so or have seen the news release from the government agency or other body.
- Avoid a flood of rhetoric. Most journalists have heard ideological arguments many times.
- Know your facts. Never offer information unless you are sure it's true. You can pass on gossip if you label it as such and are prepared to take responsibility for talking about it.
- Know where to find information fast. A reporter will call again if you earn a reputation for locating information for him or her or for suggesting another credible person to call. But don't promise to find information unless you are sure you can get it. (Don't necessarily push to be quoted if you find information for a journalist.)

Tips on Developing Credibility

- Always be accurate. Journalists turn to credible sources for accurate information. The worst move you can make is to embarrass a reporter by feeding him or her wrong information. With accuracy as a baseline, you can earn a reputation as a credible source.
- Be quoted by various outlets. Journalists look at the work of their peers, and if you're in a story they see, you establish credibility. That's one reason to make the effort to be quoted in any outlet.
- Offer information even if you don't expect to be quoted. "If the only time I hear from you is when you're pitching your

organization, that's of limited value," says Colin Covert, a feature reporter for the *Star Tribune* in Minneapolis.

- Compliment your adversaries. A journalist is trying to understand a debate. If you show him or her that you can understand different sides (though your side is right), you will earn credibility. "Activists tend to present the other side as nothing more than a pack of lies," says Paul Vamvas, a Washington, D.C.–based producer for Worldnet Television. "You should be able to argue the other side, and do it credibly."
- Don't exaggerate. It's important to present your point of view in dramatic terms, but don't overdo it. "Activists almost always start out with credibility," says Dave Blackwell, an assignment editor for KWGN-TV, an unaffiliated station in Denver. "When they cry wolf too much, it erodes."

Tips on Cultivating a
Lasting Relationship with a Journalist

- Different outlets have different deadlines. Learn them so that you don't annoy journalists near their crunch time. Generally, mornings are best for calling journalists, early in the week if possible. "The most common problem is not to think about our deadlines," says Tom Donahue, Miami bureau chief for CBS News.
- Don't bother reporters. Most busy reporters—with some exceptions—don't want you to "check in" for no reason. Call when you have something to say.
- Make life easy for reporters. Have visual images for television and newsworthy information for the print media.
- If a reporter calls you for a comment on a story, don't disclose the story to other journalists. A reporter will not be happy about losing an exclusive thanks to you.

- Refrain from thanking a journalist. It's appropriate—on rare occasions—to compliment a journalist for writing a fair and accurate piece, but hold the thank-yous because reporters, as professionals, are not aiming to please you. (You will find columnists or reporters who openly advocate your position. A thank-you call may be appropriate for them, but be wary.)
- Don't assume a journalist is your friend or your enemy. Even if a reporter writes articles sympathetic to your issue, don't assume he or she supports you or your cause. Continue to treat a reporter as a judge or observer until you have good reason to assume otherwise. Of course, it's not uncommon for journalists to become friends with their sources.
- Recognize that journalists aren't independent operators. Sometimes, editors nix their ideas for stories. "Even when someone has me completely convinced, they're only halfway home," says Peter Dykstra, a senior producer for Cable News Network in Atlanta.
- If you see a journalist in a public place or social gathering, approach him or her without being rude. Be friendly.

Tips on Keeping Your Media List Updated

- Keep track of revolving journalists, who change jobs frequently. For example, some of the reporters interviewed for this book switched jobs or quit as it was being written. Even if they stay at one publication, they often shift beats (issue areas). Sending a release to the correct education writer instead of the former one will reflect well on you as a source of information.
- Know about the rise and demise of news departments. During the course of any given year, news departments at outlets may be eliminated completely, transformed, or—less likely these days—created from scratch.

- Educate yourself about information technology. Be on the lookout for information about where people turn for their news and the news options available to them. Although the alleged explosion of the information highway may be somewhat hyped, it's definitely true that patterns of news consumption are changing. Clearly, keeping abreast of this is critical.

35

How and When to
Complain About Coverage

GOOD REPORTERS ASK GOOD QUESTIONS, and sometimes their best questions seem offensive or irrelevant. But you seldom gain anything by getting angry at a reporter. You win by answering questions *and* staying "on message."

Just as reporters must ask tough questions, it's also a reporter's job to leave you out of the news if he or she deems it appropriate to do so. Reporters are paid to weigh your "news" against other "news." Nevertheless, it's hard not to be annoyed or angry when a reporter misquotes you, writes an inaccurate story, shuts you out of the news, or offends you in some other serious way.

Despite their best efforts to be accurate, journalists make errors. They occur in news stories, editorials, columns, features, even in the food section. In his farewell column to *Denver Post* readers, food writer John Kessler wrote, "You've kept me honest through numerous gaffes. You let me know when my Chinese Orange Chicken recipe was missing a key ingredient (chicken)."[1]

With deadline pressures, reduced staffs, information overload, and other complications, it's a wonder mistakes in the news aren't more common. (For a discussion of other common limitations of news reporting, see the "headaches" listed in Chapter 29, "Publicize a Report or Academic Paper.") This means that you should expect mistakes to appear in stories that affect you and your issue. In general, keep the big picture in mind and don't get too worked up about any single error.

Tips for Complaining About Errors in Stories

• When it comes to complaining, proceed slowly. Remember, a news story is old news tomorrow and usually, by itself, insignificant in the big picture. Bothering a busy reporter about debatable "mistakes" will hurt your cause more than help it. Often, an error is a matter of interpretation. As *Rocky Mountain News* reporter Bill Scanlon put it, "Usually the mistake falls somewhere between my being totally blameless and something that requires a correction."

• If a reporter has made a significant factual error in a piece, call him or her and discuss it. There's a good chance he or she will be glad you called and will probably not make the mistake next time. Make sure you have credible documentation of your position ready to fax.

• If you don't call, the error may be repeated. At newspapers, stories are filed in an internal library, and information they contain is later used when a reporter checks library clips for background information on a new story. Don't let serious errors get institutionalized.

• Don't necessarily demand that a correction be published or aired during the broadcast. Only rarely is an error serious enough to demand a correction for the record.

• If a mistake is made repeatedly, further action on your part could be warranted. If the error is serious enough and if "the reporter's a jerk," says Janet Day, a business editor for the *Denver Post*, "call the editor." (Call the news director at TV or radio stations.)

• If your organization's activities are repeatedly shut out, call the reporter who covers your issue area and ask why. If the answer is not satisfactory and the problem is ongoing, meet with his or her superiors. But do not expect coverage every time.

- Some activists forget that the newsroom is composed of individuals. Harassing these individuals as if they were a faceless institution will set you and your cause back.
- Don't complain to the "ombudsman." Some papers have a "readers' representative" called the ombudsman. If you have a problem with newspaper coverage, you should deal directly with the journalists involved. If you've got a good argument to make, the journalists will appreciate hearing from you directly.
- Don't complain to reporters about headlines. Reporters don't write headlines, and it's often headlines that are inaccurate or misleading. You can complain to editors about headlines, but such complaints aren't worth the trouble.
- Don't complain to reporters about spelling, grammar, or printing problems. Again, this is the responsibility of the editors and is better left for retired librarians to worry about.
- Don't complain about a reporter who shows up late to your event, quotes citizens who know nothing about the issue, leaves out information about how people can contact you or how they can attend a meeting, or chooses an unflattering quote. None of these "errors," especially if they are not part of a documentable pattern, merit your complaints.

Reporters are people with strengths and faults. Sometimes, I find myself expecting too much of them, maybe because I think their job is so important. But then I remind myself that they are regular working people, sometimes enjoying their jobs, sometimes not. You can gain some insight into the life of journalists if you watch them when they are not swarming around a press conference or sitting across from you at an interview. If there is a media frenzy in your area, take an hour and observe the journalists during "downtime," when they're waiting for a news conference, eating lunch, or hanging around the entrance to the courthouse. You'll see ordinary people—not a bunch of mini–Sam Donaldsons. Most of them are struggling to figure things out just like everybody else.

Here's an anecdote to illustrate: I once organized a rally to oppose the "media frenzy" around the murder of a child named JonBenét Ramsey in Boulder, Colorado. The national media had been covering the Ramsey murder in force. About twenty journalists showed up. For the most part, they covered the rally accurately and with sensitivity. (Many journalists were as sick of covering the story as our group was of reading about it.)

As we were packing up our signs to leave, one photographer with a huge camera asked if she could have one of our signs, which depicted a red-eyed black vulture with the word "TeleVulture" beneath it. I said, "Sure, please, have it," and I gave it to her. As I was leaving, I saw her holding the TeleVulture sign above her head as another photographer took her photograph.

You could look at this photographer as another thoughtless journalist who thinks it's funny to be called a televulture (it is, actually). But I think it's more accurate to think of her this way: She's a person trying to make the best out of a difficult job—often with low pay and lousy hours—and trying to find humor and enjoyment in it.

36

Organize to Demand
Better Journalism

Despite widespread distrust of journalists and unhappiness with the news, few people take action—much less organize—to demand better journalism. Think of a worthy cause—from homelessness to the ozone layer—and you can probably name five nonprofit organizations working on the problem. But how many citizens' groups have been established to demand fair and accurate journalism from news outlets? Few.

Why the absence of "media activism"? First, the quality of the news is at once everybody's concern and nobody's. You don't see people organizing to improve journalism like they might to stop a toxic waste dump in their neighborhood. Bad journalism doesn't present the kind of immediate threat to people's self-interests that, for better or worse, inspires most activism.

Even when poor-quality journalism does fire people up enough to elicit action, it's hard for citizens to identify a target for their hostility. Which commercial media outlet is responsible for the latest courthouse frenzy? For the O. J. Simpson fixation? Which local TV news program serves up the most mayhem and fluff?

In addition, people are skeptical about citizen activism in general; they don't believe any action by citizens will affect giant media corporations that are happy with their profits. (Ben Bagdikian's *Media Monopoly* explains how ownership of the news

235

media is increasingly concentrated in the hands of fewer and fewer large corporations.)

Citizens understand that mainstream news outlets, like other large corporations, are not required to care much about their communities or employees. And although we want the government to force corporations to produce safe cars, we don't want regulators telling media corporations what's news. Potential media activists become paralyzed when asked, "Do you want the government deciding what's news?"

Potential media activists are also stymied by the defense, offered by some journalists, that news corporations simply give the people what they want—never mind the obvious role the mass media have in determining what people want in the first place. And some activists wisely believe that it's not worth criticizing the media, because if they do, there's even less of a chance journalists will cover the issues they are concerned about.

So what can we do? The half of us who chose to vote in the last election—and the half who didn't—need better journalism.

If you're an advocate for a cause, you should probably be cautious about criticizing the media too much for fear of alienating journalists from talking to you about your issue. But there are actions you can take, and at a minimum, you can encourage others to talk back to the news media.

Tips for Demanding Better News

- Don't yell at the television in the dark. Complain to journalists directly by phone or letter. You can also write a letter to the editor. This can work. For example, an activist in Denver was outraged that a local TV station chose to feature on its 5 P.M. broadcast a small scuffle in a story about a large Martin Luther King Day parade. She called the station, and the scuffle was downplayed on the often-more-sensational 10 P.M. show.

- Call media outlets with story ideas. Many journalists want to hear from reasonable citizens. Your news may bump the latest trivial crime video from reaching the living rooms of hundreds of thousands of people.
- Join a media watchdog group. Clearly, these groups will be more effective if they develop large constituencies, especially because few foundations support media activism. (See Chapter 40, "News Media Watchdog Groups.")
- Seek and *promote* alternative news. Diverse sources of news are plentiful in this country, but few people tune in.
- Talk about the quality of news. What constitutes responsible journalism? Debate this on talk radio or on the Internet.
- Track issues that concern you. Let news outlets know how they are covering the issues that matter most to you.

If you're a more motivated media activist, you can document your concerns about news coverage over time and present them to journalists in a report. Often this is a more effective way to criticize the news than complaining about an isolated story, because most professional journalists strive for balance and fairness; when documentation shows that their work is otherwise, they take notice. The best media-activist organizations produce reports that objectively document their criticisms of the news media.

Examples of Reports by Media Activists

The Freedom Forum, based in Virginia, conducted a study of the front pages of twenty newspapers for one month, demonstrating that although women make up 52 percent of the population, they account for only 15 percent of front-page news coverage.

Fairness and Accuracy in Reporting (FAIR), based in New York, has released numerous studies quantifying its criticisms about the news media. One 1989 report documented that about

90 percent of guests on the *MacNeil/Lehrer News Hour* were white and 87 percent of them were male. A similar FAIR study of *Nightline* showed that 89 percent of its guests were white and 82 percent, male. Another exhaustive report on Rush Limbaugh, titled *The Way Things Aren't: Rush Limbaugh's Reign of Error*, documented factual errors in Limbaugh's commentary.

The Center for Communication and Social Policy at the University of California, Santa Barbara, categorized violent acts on prime time television and documented that only 4 percent of programs with violence had an antiviolence theme, which was defined as a focus on alternatives to violence or on the pain and suffering of victims.

Rocky Mountain Media Watch, a media-activist nonprofit that I cofounded, also analyzes the news media. Our annual "snapshot" studies of about 100 newscasts in over fifty U.S. cities on one evening show that crime coverage eats up about 30 percent of local TV news around the country—even at a time when crime rates are dropping. More time is dedicated to chatter between anchors than to stories about the environment, and some stations have more commercials than news. Soft news, such as "pelican gets beak treatment," "hypnosis for horses," "beauty contest for cows," "principal eats worm," and "100th anniversary of Jell-O," receives more coverage than education, AIDS, children, and most other subjects you can think of.

Steps for Documenting Bias in the News

Step 1.   Identify a problem in the media that you want to highlight. (Example: Our organization, Rocky Mountain Media Watch, noted that there appeared to be few opinion columns written by guests—members of the community—in our local papers. The pundits seemed to be mostly nationally known writers whose work appears in newspapers across the United States.)

Step 2. Devise a plan to show—quantifiably and objectively—that the "problem" you're concerned about exists. (Example: We decided to count how many op-eds by guest writers appeared in our local papers over a one-month period. We called it our Pundit Watch project.)

Step 3. Conduct your research and compile your results. (Example: It turned out that during our sample period, 11 percent of columns in the *Denver Post* and 7 percent in the *Rocky Mountain News* were written by guests.)

Step 4. Write a short report about your results. Take time to present your data clearly and include recommendations for improvement. (Example: We wrote a three-page report entitled "Choices of Voices: The Op-Ed Pages of Denver Newspapers." Among other recommendations, we called on the editorial page editors to publish a substantial number of columns by guests.)

Step 5. Send your report to relevant journalists with a request for a meeting. Follow up with a phone call if necessary. (Example: We had a half-hour phone conversation with the editorial page editor of the *News* and met in person with the *Post*'s editorial page editor.)

Step 6. Consider publicizing your results. Depending on how your meetings with journalists go, you may want to try to generate news coverage of your report. (Example: We pitched our report to talk-radio shows and alternative print publications. The *Denver Business Journal*, a local business paper, and *Westword*, our city's major alternative paper, covered our study. We were also guests on two prominent talk-radio shows. And we were attacked by regular columnists for bean counting.)

Step 7. Assess your results. If you are not satisfied with the response to your report, consider stepping up your organizing efforts. Would other groups endorse your report? Would citizens turn out for a demonstration? (Example: We repeated our study for two years, and recently the *Post* announced it would reserve space for a weekly column by a guest. We plan to repeat the study again.)

Step 8. Consider expanding your focus. Could you include other news media outlets and make your study national? (Example: In our most recent report, we analyzed seven newspapers from around the United States, including national newspapers such as the *New York Times*. We did not find that guests were lacking, but our data revealed a pundit gender gap: Seventy-five percent of opinion columns nationally were written by men. We received a bit of national attention for our work as well.)

The initial efforts of media activists may have minimal impact, perhaps affecting only a handful of news decisions over many years. But the mainstream news media, particularly television, are too powerful to ignore. And our democratic society depends on responsible, informative journalism.

Part Five

How to Develop a Strategy to Win Your Campaign

THIS BOOK IS ABOUT how to get media attention, not how to win your campaign or how to achieve something—except making the news. If you don't have a strategy to guide your work, you should develop one. I've included the following chapter to help you begin thinking about a strategy. Chapter 43, "Community Organizing and Fundraising Information," describes some resources that may be useful to you as you further develop your strategy.

37

Landing on *Oprah*
Is Not a Strategy

SOME PEOPLE CRITICIZE nonprofits and activists because they think our goal—above all else—is to get on TV or on the front page of the newspaper (or any page, for that matter). Criticism of activists whose *only* goal is to catch the attention of Oprah or the ten o'clock news is, of course, justified. Many activists flail around without thinking through how they are actually going to solve the problem they are worried about. Some think media coverage is an end in itself.

It isn't. Efforts to land in the news should be connected to a larger strategy about how to gain a political victory or make some substantive progress on a specific issue or cause.

In the long term, your work with the news media should be guided, in part, by how you want your organization and issue to be perceived by citizens. Media outreach should be part of a long-term communications plan, covering all aspects of your organization's public profile (speeches, flyers, posters, events, newsletters, alerts, fundraising appeals, and so on). Your communications plan should answer the question: How do you want to shape public opinion about your issue and organization? (For a thoughtful discussion of this, read *How to Tell and Sell Your Story*, listed in Chapter 38.) In the short term, manipulating the media to cover an issue is a tool, one tool among many, that an activist

243

has available. This tool should be used thoughtfully to maximize its impact.

After you study an issue, it may turn out that instead of focusing scarce energy or dollars on a media event (or media outreach of any kind), it makes more sense to expend your resources elsewhere—say, to hire a lawyer. To determine how to best allocate resources, ask yourself, Which decisionmakers have to act? For example, can the governor single-handedly allay your concerns? Does the mayor have the ultimate power? Perhaps the buck stops at the city council or the air-quality commission or the school board.

Once you've identified which decisionmakers have to act, ask yourself, How can they be influenced? There are as many strategies to influence a decisionmaker as there are creative minds to think of them. Common strategies can be divided into four categories: legal, electoral, consumer, and lobbying. (A campaign may engage in all simultaneously.) Each of these may or may not have a media component.

Legal Strategies

A legal strategy, which can be costly, usually involves filing or threatening to file a lawsuit to force some sort of action or inaction. For example, the Natural Resources Defense Council, an environmental group, filed a lawsuit in 1991 contending that the federal government needed a permit from the state of New Mexico before dumping radioactive waste there. A district court judge agreed and issued an order blocking shipments of waste to the dump until the permit was issued.

A media campaign may be a useful component of a legal strategy, depending on your (or your lawyer's) assessment of how the judge will respond to media coverage. Sometimes lawsuits are threatened or filed simply to attract media attention, pushing other decisionmakers—perhaps in the legislature—to act. In this case, a lawsuit is a lobbying tool.

Electoral Strategies

There are two typical kinds of electoral strategies: The first is to ensure that sympathetic politicians are elected to the decision-making posts that will affect your cause. (Citizens do this by helping a political campaign.) The second is to organize a ballot initiative allowing citizens directly to vote into law a measure addressing your concern. Political campaigns and citizens' ballot initiatives try to use the news media in support of their candidates or ballot measures.

Consumer Strategies: Boycotts and Girlcotts

By attacking carefully cultivated corporate images and by organizing citizens to refuse to buy targeted products, activists try to influence decisions by corporations. There are about 200 consumer boycotts in progress in the United States.

Whereas the efficacy of most boycotts can be seriously questioned, a successful boycott can be a landmark victory for a cause. Boycotts can also be particularly effective against small, local companies.

Conversely, activists sometimes choose to acknowledge good behavior by encouraging citizens to buy targeted products. This is called a girlcott. For example, New Zealand activists tried to boost the resolve of their political leaders concerning the ban on nuclear-armed ships. They called on citizens around the world to buy "New Zealand nuclear free" products such as kiwifruit.

Boycotters and girlcotters try to use the media to get the word out about their cause. Sometimes activists use the threat of a boycott or call for a boycott with the intention of garnering media coverage that will push other decisionmakers (e.g., a mayor) to act.

Lobbying Strategies

When most people think of lobbying, they think of smoky back rooms with piles of $100 bills stacked on tables. At the least, most people associate lobbying with large money transfers. But cash contributions are only one type of lobbying. Other approaches include locating someone who has a personal relationship with the decisionmaker you want to influence; persuading the staff of the relevant decisionmaker to support your cause; backing the appointment of sympathetic officials to key decisionmaking positions; commissioning scientific or legal experts to support your cause with technical information; and activating the constituents of a decisionmaker (even of an advertiser) to apply pressure (letters, calls, telegrams, faxes, visits).

Generating media coverage about a political cause is a public form of lobbying. It derives its power from its public nature and its ability to embarrass. Once a political message is absorbed in the media, it is transformed from a private gripe to a public concern. It can suddenly be endowed with the moral force of an "audience" of nameless constituents who have the potential to cast public shame on a decisionmaker (such as a state legislator or other elected official) or vote him or her out of office.

In deciding how to deal with an issue that has been in the media, politicians have to cope with the fact that voters may have heard about it and that a percentage of them may care about it and expect action. Also, decisionmakers are aware that once an issue is in the public arena, their political opponents are more likely to point to it as a "failure" if nothing is done about it.

Overall, to an official's mind, an issue that is in the media is a land mine. Politicians usually try to avoid even the most remote chance of public condemnation—particularly from their middle-of-the-road constituency.

But lobbying through the mainstream media may also have the opposite effect. Some decisionmakers may react so negatively to efforts to shine the media spotlight on them that they will specifically *not* do what you want them to do.

Remember that although a decisionmaker may not respond favorably to a hard-hitting media strategy, he or she will probably remember you're out there the next time a similar issue arises. Thus your efforts might pay off in the longer term.

Depending on your strategy, a media event targeting a specific decisionmaker might make sense only after low-profile lobbying tactics (meetings, letter writing) have failed. A gentle media event (a low-key rally) could be followed up by a more confrontational one (a sit-in at his or her office). Or you might want to devise a media campaign that, instead of making demands of only one decisionmaker, focuses on publicizing the problem in general or calls on a group of politicians to take action. Another approach is to scapegoat one decisionmaker who will never support you, knowing that your real target is another decisionmaker.

Although it is important to try to determine how publicizing your cause fits into your grand plan of how to solve it, it is naive to think that your campaign will proceed as planned. The evolution of almost all policy debates is replete with surprises. There is no way to predict exactly how a community issue will be resolved. Often something falls from the blue, and suddenly everything has changed.

As a result, all strategies must be flexible. A media campaign may be wrong today but right tomorrow. You may have decided a month ago that filing a lawsuit was the best way to get the results you want and that lobbying was a waste of time. But now the county commissioners have resigned over a scandal and lobbying—with a media component—looks cheaper and more promising.

You will sometimes be unsure whether a media campaign will be useful. If you're in doubt, go ahead. It's true that a media campaign can be counterproductive. This is rare, especially if it is well conceived. You can hedge your bet by refining your message, dealing effectively with reporters, and orchestrating the types of media events that will be less damaging if there is a problem.

Also, media attention usually opens more doors than it closes. It tends to make things happen. You're in the paper and you get a call from a citizen who has been trying to do something about the same problem for years. Someone else reads about your efforts and secretly leaks you vital information. Volunteers appear from the woodwork. Someone drops a $5,000 check in your mailbox.

Media attention can be one of the cheapest tools an activist has available. You can generate hundreds of thousands of dollars' worth of free airtime for a cause by organizing a media event costing under $10. Taking advantage of free media is a powerful tactic to change the world.

Part Six

Resources

38

Media How-to Books

Most large advocacy groups produce media guides about their issue for internal use. They're usually very helpful because they address the media nuances of specific issues. I've seen the internal work of the American Federation of State, County, and Municipal Employees; the American Israel Public Affairs Committee; the Citizens Clearinghouse for Hazardous Waste; Greenpeace; the Nature Conservancy; Planned Parenthood; the Ruckus Society; the Safe Energy Communications Council; and the Wilderness Society. Ask a national organization that works on your issue if it has its own guide.

There are few books written for activists and nonprofit organizations that focus exclusively on the news media. You should look at any you can find.

Strategic Communication for Nonprofits (1992)
Larry Kirkman and Karen Menichelli, Editors
The Benton Foundation
1634 I Street, 12th Floor
Washington, DC 20006
The Benton Foundation has published a series of booklets providing in-depth yet relatively accessible information on media access for nonprofit organizations. They are an excellent resource. The titles of the publications in the series are *Talk Radio, Voice Programs, Op-Eds, Using Video, Media Advocacy, Cable Access, Electronic Networking,* and *Independent Features.*

Media How-to Guidebook (1991)
David Perry
San Francisco Media Alliance
814 Mission Street, #295
San Francisco, CA 94103
The *Media How-to Guidebook* is a well-organized, concise hand-book, appropriately titled. Make sure you buy this one even though it's a bit dated.

The Jossey-Bass Guide to Strategic Communications for Nonprofits (1998)
Kathy Bonk, Henry Griggs, and Emily Tynes
Josey-Bass Publishers
San Francisco, CA
A comprehensive book with tips on how to use new communications tools and much more. Valuable.

Media Advocacy and Public Health (1993)
Lawrence Wallack, Lori Dorfman, David Jernigan, and Makani Themba
Sage Publications
Thousand Oaks, CA
Media Advocacy and Public Health focuses on how to devise media strategies and messages to advance policy goals. Its focus is public health policy, but the information could be used by any advocate. If you can't muster the commitment to read it all, check out Chapter 4, "Thinking Media Advocacy," and Chapter 6, "Media Advocacy Case Studies."

The Activist Cookbook (1997)
Andrew Boyd
United for a Fair Economy
37 Temple Place, 5th Floor
Boston, MA 02111

A great resource for helping you think creatively about media events and involving artists in your work. Don't miss the list of resources at the end of this manual.

How to Tell and Sell Your Story (1997)
Timothy Saasta
Center for Community Change
1000 Wisconsin Avenue NW
Washington, DC 20007
A thoughtful booklet about media outreach, especially for issues related to low-income housing. A second volume, published in 1998, contains excellent advice on how to develop effective messages, in part by using low-budget polls and focus groups.

Prime Time Activism (1991)
Charlotte Ryan
South End Press
Boston, MA
Prime Time Activism is both a progressive academic analysis of the news media and a guide to help activists manipulate the news. It's a dense read for a busy practitioner, but there are lots of interesting ideas here, particularly if you're interested in theory.

We Interrupt This Program: A Citizen's Guide to Using the Media for Social Change (1978)
Robbie Gordon
Citizens Involvement Training Project
School of Education
University of Massachusetts
464 Hills South
Amherst, MA 01003
This is a pioneering, comprehensive work that's quite dated now but still worth reading.

How You Can Manipulate the Media (1993)
David Alexander
Paladin Press
Boulder, CO
Some of the media tips in *How You Can Manipulate the Media,*
such as lying to the media, should be ignored. But it's still inter-
esting to read the descriptions of some of the unusual media
stunts.

Resources for Non-Profits
Chronicle of Philanthropy, Annual
Applied Research and Development International
2121 South Oneida Street, Suite 633
Denver, CO 80224
An extensive annual compilation of resources available for
nonprofits, including books, periodicals, and consulting services.
Sections on advocacy and marketing contain media-related re-
sources, but all aspects of nonprofit management are covered:
ethics, human resources, legal issues, planning, and more.

Nonprofit World
The Society for Nonprofit Organizations
6314 Odana Road, Suite 1
Madison, WI 53719
Nonprofit World is a bimonthly magazine that contains useful
information about the media, marketing, fund-raising, and other
concerns of nonprofit organizations.

There are good media how-to books written more for businesspeople than for nonprofits and activists. But many of the same
principles apply (e.g., news releases, interviews, news conferences). Some of these books follow.

Dealing Effectively with the Media (1992)
John Wade
Crisp Publications

Menlo Park, CA
Dealing Effectively with the Media focuses on interviews. It offers some excellent interview tricks and preparation ideas. Definitely worth buying.

The Executive's Guide to Handling a Press Interview (1990)
Dick Martin
Pilot Industries
103 Cooper Street
Babylon, NY 11702
The forty-seven-page *Executive's Guide* is filled with amusing examples of how businesses have successfully—and unsuccessfully—interacted with the news media. Its tips are good, too.

The Publicity Handbook (1991)
David R. Yale
NTC Business Books
Lincolnwood, IL
This book is so comprehensive you're bound to learn something if you read it.

You'll find a stack of general books on marketing in the library. It's worth perusing them for an hour on a rainy afternoon. Most are written for small businesses and entrepreneurs, covering not just the news media but advertising, flyers, business cards, newsletters, direct mail, speeches, canvassing, personal calls, and more. One book to look for:

Guerilla Marketing (1993)
Jay Conrad Levinson
Houghton Mifflin
New York, NY
Levinson's series of books deserves the wide attention it has garnered.

39

Sources for Lists
of News Outlets

THE BEST WAY TO OBTAIN A MEDIA LIST is to borrow one from
an allied organization that works on your issue. If you seek a list
of media in your community, a local group is probably best because it would presumably interact with local journalists, but national organizations often have good local media lists as well.
Otherwise, start your list by reviewing a reference book in the library or buying your own reference book or CD-ROM. (See
Chapter 8, "Compile a Media List.")

Many states have at least one association of nonprofit organizations. These associations are composed of nonprofits that pay
membership dues in exchange for benefits such as reduced rates
on health insurance, free seminars, tax information, and legisla-
tive tracking. You should be able to obtain the name and address
of your local association by contacting a national association of
nonprofit organizations.

Bacon's Media Directories
322 South Michigan Avenue
Chicago, IL 60604
Bacon's publishes a series of voluminous media directories for
newspapers, magazines, radio, TV/cable, international media,
and so on.

Working Press of the Nation
National Register Publishing
New Providence, NJ
This three-volume set, updated annually, contains detailed information on print and broadcast outlets—including names of reporters and editors—across the country.

Alternative Press Index
Alternative Press Center
Box 33109
Baltimore, MD 21218
Available in both print and CD-ROM formats, this is widely regarded as the leading guide to the alternative press in North America. You would probably not want to buy this quarterly subject index, but look at it at the library to upgrade your list of alternative news outlets that cover your issue.

Alliance for Community Media
666 11th Street NW, Suite 806
Washington, DC 20001
This group publishes a directory of community media centers across the United States. These centers house cable-access channels or other media-access services available to the public.

National Council of Nonprofit Associations
1001 Connecticut Avenue
Washington, DC 20036
The National Council is the umbrella alliance of state and regional associations of nonprofit groups and represents thousands of individual nonprofits. It provides services and networking. Find out if your state or region has an association of nonprofit organizations.

40

News Media Watchdog Groups

Accuracy in Media (AIM)
1275 K Street NW
Washington, DC 20005
Probably the leading conservative news watchdog organization. If you've read this book, you know I don't share much of AIM's politics—or its belief that the news media have a liberal bias—but I think it's worthwhile to keep an eye on its publications and activities. I find that both liberal and conservative media critics share a disdain for tabloid news and sensationalism in the news. Both want more substantive information. Both hate local TV news shows.

Adbusters
c/o The Media Foundation
1243 West 7th Avenue
Vancouver, BC V6H 1B7
Canada
http://www.adbusters.org.adbusters/
The Media Foundation publishes a fantastic quarterly magazine called *Adbusters,* which criticizes the news media, promotes media activism, and mocks popular advertisements. The staff creates advertisements of its own, which it tries to place in main-

stream publications. It also consults with activists on the creation of advertisements. Be a "culture jammer" and subscribe to *Adbusters*.

The Benton Foundation
1634 I Street, 12th Floor
Washington, DC 20006
http://www.benton.org
Helps citizens access the news media and promotes "media in the public interest."

Environmental Media Services
1606 20th Street NW, 2nd Floor
Washington, DC 20009
An effective organization that promotes media coverage of environmental issues.

Fairness and Accuracy in Reporting (FAIR)
130 West 25th Street
New York, NY 10001
http://www.fair.org/fair/
The leading progressive news watchdog organization. FAIR publishes *EXTRA!*, a bimonthly magazine focusing on the news media, and produces *Counterspin*, a national radio show about the news media. FAIR has documented convincingly that the mainstream media have a conservative—not a liberal—bias. It provides great resources and assistance—including lots of good information on the Internet—to citizens who want to initiate campaigns critical of the news media.

Independent Media Institute
  (formerly Institute for Alternative Journalism)
77 Federal Street
San Francisco, CA 94107
http://www.alternet.org/an/

The IAJ aims to strengthen alternative journalism and improve the public's access to information. Its Web site contains Media-Culture, featuring commentary and criticism about the media. It also has a project, called Strategic Progressive Information Network (SPIN), that helps progressive activists with their media outreach efforts.

Media Research Center
113 South West Street
Alexandria, VA 22314
http://www.pff.org/mrc/
A conservative media research and activist organization. Publishes a newsletter.

National Campaign for Freedom of Expression
918 F Street Northwest #609
Washington, D.C. 20004
Monitors censorship of artistic expression in the news and elsewhere. Publishes a great quarterly newsletter filled with information about new resources and efforts to censor art.

Project Censored
1801 Cotati Avenue
Sonoma State University
Rohnert Park, CA 94928
Find out from this group what the national media do *not* cover. Its annual report is always a refreshing and illuminating read.

Rocky Mountain Media Watch
Box 18858
Denver, CO 80218
303-832-7558
http://www.imagepage.com/rmmw/index.html

Based in Denver, this nonprofit, which I cofounded, monitors local news media, particularly local TV news. It writes reports such as "Baaad News: Local TV News in America" and "Choices of Voices: Op-Ed Writers in U.S. Newspapers"; sponsors protests, for example, a 1997 rally in Boulder opposing the JonBenét Ramsey media frenzy; and writes articles and commentaries about the news.

Tyndall Report
135 Rivington Street
New York, NY 10002
A thorough and credible research organization. Write for content analyses of national network news shows.

Center for Commercial-Free Public Education
360 Grand Avenue
Box 385
Oakland, CA 94610
Fights attempts to commercialize the classroom.

41

Media Literacy Organizations

Center for Media Education
1511 K Street NW, Suite 518
Washington, DC 20005
http://www.tap.epn.org/cme/sitemap
Conducts research and promotes policy relating to, among other subjects, TV programming for children.

Center for Media Literacy
4727 Wilshire Boulevard., Suite 403
Los Angeles, CA 90010
http://www.medialit.org/
Write for an extensive catalog of media education resources.

The Children's Television Resource and Education Center
340 Townsend Street
San Francisco, CA 94107
Focuses on issues related to children and television.

Mediascope
12711 Ventura Boulevard., Suite 280
Studio City, CA 91604
http://www.mediascope.org/mediascope

Promotes ratings for television shows, allowing parents and citizens to anticipate the content of programming for themselves and their children.

Media Watch
Box 618
Santa Cruz, CA 95061-0618
This organization, which aims in part to improve the image of women in the media, has produced popular videos titled *Warning: The Media May Be Hazardous to Your Health* and *Don't Be a TV-Television Victim.*

National Institute on Media and the Family
2450 Riverside Avenue
Minneapolis, MN 55454
http://www.media and the family.org
Publishes a newsletter, *Unplug Your Kids,* and coordinates other projects on the impact of the media on children.

PR WATCH
3318 Gregory Street
Madison, WI 53711
Publishes an excellent quarterly newsletter illuminating the manipulative ways of the PR industry.

TV-Free America
1611 Connecticut Avenue NW
Washington, DC 20009
http://www.essential.org/orgs/tvfa
This organization's goal is to encourage U.S. citizens to reduce their consumption of TV. It sponsors TV-Turnoff Week, which is popular among teachers concerned about the tube. Turning off the TV for a week is an excellent way to understand the power of television. Try it.

42

Communications
Consultants

COMMUNICATIONS CONSULTANTS provide different services
for nonprofit organizations, including product and service marketing, media relations (to generate news coverage), logo design,
message development, advertising (to develop and place ads),
event planning, desktop publishing (to produce newsletters, reports, etc.), direct mail, conference planning, photodocumenta-
tion, speech writing, and strategic communications consulting. If
you hire a communications consultant, make sure your needs
match his or her strengths. Some provide services pro-bono.

American Forum
529 14th Street NW
Washington, DC 20045
Helps organizations place op-eds and other articles in news
outlets, particularly in the southern United States.

Berkeley Media Studies Group
2140 Shattuck Avenue, #804
Berkeley, CA 94704
Specializes in helping community groups working on public
health issues use the media strategically.

Cause Communications
1836 Blake Street, Suite 100B
Denver, CO 80202
A company founded by the author of this book. Provides
workshops and consulting services to nonprofit organizations
and concerned citizens.

Center for Strategic Communications
72 Spring Street, Suite 208
New York, NY 10012
Provides an array of publications and services, including media workshops.

Communications Consortium
1333 H Street NW, #700
Washington, DC 20005
Particularly interested in helping coalitions of progressive,
nonprofit groups access the media.

Communications Works
2017 Mission Street, Suite 303
San Francisco, CA 94110
Media consulting services for progressive organizations.

Fenton Communications
1606 20th Street NW
Washington, DC 20009
Public interest media consulting.

McKinney & Dowell Associates
1325 G Street NW
Washington, DC 20005
General media consulting and services for progressive groups.

ProMedia
225 West 57th Street, Suite 801
New York, NY 10019
Public interest media consulting.

Public Media Center
466 Green Street
San Francisco, CA 94133
A great resource for nonprofits that want to make a splash with creative, hard-hitting advertisements.

Public Policy Communications
73 Towbridge Street
Belmont, MA 02178
Excellent strategy and media advice.

Riptide Communications
666 Broadway, Room 625
New York, NY 10012
Public interest media consulting.

Safe Energy Communications Council
1717 Massachusetts Avenue
Washington, DC 20036
Offers workshops on publicizing issues related to energy policy.

The Progressive Media Project
409 East Main Street
Madison, WI 53703
This is not really a communications consulting organization, but it doesn't fit in any of the other resource categories I've got in this book. It helps you publish your opinion article in mainstream newspapers across the country. This is a great way to help activists get the word out.

The Spin Project
77 Federal Street
San Francisco, CA 94107
Offers media workshops and strategizing for progressive organizations. Useful resources including some media lists, can be found on its web site: www.mediademocracy.org/spin.

Vanguard Communications
1019 19th Street NW
Washington, DC 20036
Focuses on providing media services to nonprofits.

43

Community Organizing and Fund-raising Information

Advocacy Institute
1707 L Street NW, #400
Washington, DC 20036
Supports and lobbies for not-for-profit initiatives. Also trains nonprofit groups.

Chronicle of Philanthropy
1255 23rd Street NW
Washington, DC 20037
Fortnightly newspaper covering the nonprofit sector, particularly fund-raising.

Enough Is Enough: How to Organize a Successful Campaign for Change (1994)
Diane Maceachern
Avon Books
New York, NY
Well-organized, user-friendly book about community organizing.

Focus on the Family
Box 35500
Colorado Springs, CO 80935

Keep an eye on what the right wing is up to by tracking this ultraconservative organization.

The Foundation Center
79 5th Avenue
New York, NY 10003
Fund-raising, organizing, marketing, and other information for nonprofits.

Fundraising for Social Change (1994)
Kim Klein
Chardon Press
Inverness, CA
Believe it or not, this is lively reading—a great tool to help energize your fund-raising efforts. Kim Klein also publishes a newsletter titled *Grassroots Fundraising Journal*. Write Box 11607, Berkeley, CA, 94701.

Highlander Center
1959 Highlander Way
New Market, TN 37820
Resources and classes on community organizing and "education for social change."

Midwest Academy
225 Ohio, Suite 250
Chicago, IL 60610
A training institute for organizers.

National Organizers' Alliance
715 G Street SE
Washington, DC 20003
Networking and services for community organizers.

Organizing for Social Change (1991)
Kim Bobo, Jackie Kendall, Steve Max
Seven Locks Press
Cabin John, MD
A comprehensive book on organizing with good tips on developing a strategy and campaign.

44

Further Reading on Media and Culture

The Media Monopoly (1983, 1997)
Ben Bagdikian
Beacon Press
Boston, MA
A seminal book spotlighting the dangers of control of the media by an increasingly small number of corporations.

The Chomsky Trilogy (1994)
David Barsamian's Interviews with Noam Chomsky
Odonian Press
Tucson, AZ
A readable summary of Chomsky's opinions. David Barsamian's weekly radio program *Alternative Radio,* aired on many community radio stations, frequently addresses issues relating to the news media.

Adventures in Medialand (1993)
Jeff Cohen and Normon Solomon
Common Courage Press
New York, NY
An entertaining and educational compilation of columns on media issues.

Breaking the News: How the Media Undermine American Democracy (1996)
James Fallows
Pantheon Books
New York, NY
Great insights on the evils of elite pundits.

Manufacturing Consent: The Political Economy of the Mass Media (1988)
Edward S. Herman and Noam Chomsky
St. Martins Press
New York, NY
Explains, among other ideas, the concept of censorship by consensus.

On Bended Knee (1988)
Mark Hertsgaard
Farrar Straus Giroux
New York, NY
An incredible analysis of the Reagan administration's PR machine. The interviews in this book will amaze you.

Abbie Hoffman: American Rebel (1993)
Marty Jezer
Rutgers University Press
New Brunswick, NJ
An engaging, critical biography of a great manipulator of the news media.

Pranks! Devious Deeds and Mischievous Mirth (1987)
Andrea Juno and V. Vale Eds.
V/Search Publications
San Francisco, CA
A one-of-a kind compilation of artistic stunts, many involving media manipulation.

Spin Cycle: Inside the Clinton Propaganda Machine (1998)
Howard Kurtz

The Free Press
New York, NY
Describes how the Clinton administration combated and manipulated the news media.

Four Arguments for the Elimination of Television (1977)
Jerry Mander
William Morrow
New York, NY
Mander details the evils of the tube. Another book by Mander, *In the Absence of the Sacred*, takes a broader swipe at the evils of technology.

The Age of Missing Information (1992)
Bill McKibben
Random House
New York, NY
An interesting comparison of TV and nature.

Understanding Media: The Extensions of Man (1964)
Marshall McLuhan
McGraw-Hill
New York, NY
A classic by the famous media critic.

Market-driven Journalism: Let the Citizen Beware (1994)
John H. McManus
Sage Publications
Thousand Oaks, CA
An insider's view of local television news.

Inventing Reality: The Politics of the Mass Media (1986)
Michael Parenti
St. Martins Press
New York, NY
Analyzes the power of the media to influence perception.

How to Watch TV News (1992)
Neil Postman and Steve Powers
Penguin Books
New York, NY
An outstanding analysis of the manipulative power of local TV news. Don't miss it.

The New Citizenship: Unconventional Politics, Activism, and Service (1997)
Craig A. Rimmerman
Westview Press
Boulder, CO
Discusses new, nontraditional ways citizens are participating in U.S. politics—and the implications for our representative democracy.

The More You Watch, the Less You Know (1997)
Danny Schechter
Seven Stories Press
New York, NY
This book dissects the mainstream media and calls for reform.

Reporters and Officials (1973)
Leon V. Sigal
D. C. Heath and Company
Lexington, MA
A classic book about the relationship between journalists and their sources.

Unplugging the Plug-in Drug (1987)
Marie Winn
Penguin Books
New York, NY
Good tips to get kids away from the TV.

45

Brief Descriptions of Staffing at Major News Outlets

Daily Newspapers

Most U.S. cities have only one major local daily newspaper. It's usually owned by a large corporation, which appoints a publisher. The executive editor is the top manager under the publisher. Depending on its size, its news department—which is managed on a day-to-day basis by the managing editor—may have national, foreign, city (or "metro"), business, features, sports, Sunday magazine, and photo editors, each of whom may have reporters working under him or her. Typically, reporters cover "beats" such as education, environment, religion, legal affairs, capitol, and others. If reporters don't cover a beat, they're often called "general assignment" reporters.

A newspaper's editors have different management responsibilities. For example, the national editor may manage "bureaus" in different cities. Each bureau might have one or more reporters. The features editor may manage lower-level editors covering food, fashion, movies, travel, and entertainment.

In addition, most dailies have an editorial page editor, who reports to the publisher. Under him or her are the editorial writers, the op-ed page columnists, the cartoonist, and the editor of the Sunday commentary pages. Also, there's the "business" side of the paper, with departments such as circulation, advertising, and personnel.

Weekly or Monthly Publications

Weeklies and monthlies are also owned by a publisher, who may or may not preside over day-to-day operations. If not, the day-to-day management duties may be assigned to an editor in chief. The top editor may work with a managing editor, who manages staff writers and freelancers. At a magazine, the top editor may have "senior" editors working under him. Advertising and circulation managers are also key personnel.

Local and National Television News

Local TV stations typically have a chain of command consisting of a president, general manager, and station manager. (Sometimes a couple of these positions are rolled into one.) Under the station manager are managers of various departments, including sales/advertising, business, community relations, program, and news. Producers, directors, writers, and the production crew report to the program manager. Anchors and assignment editors report to the news director; reporters and news producers are under the assignment editor.

National networks have a news division, presided over by a president. Generally, correspondents or reporters, producers and anchors, report to executive producers.

TV Public Affairs Programs and National TV Talk Shows and News Magazines

At local television stations, producers are in charge of public affairs programs. Producers typically report to the program manager. At the national level, producers for specific shows report to an executive producer. The on-air personalities have varying degrees of involvement in program content.

News, Talk, and Pop Radio

The station manager is the boss at a radio station. The news director, who may report to the program manager, is often the lone employee in the news department, if a radio station has a news department at all. Most local stations don't. At national radio networks such as CBS Radio Network and National Public Radio, reporters work for producers or news directors.

Talk-show hosts and producers typically report to the program manager, who's under the station manager. DJs on pop radio also report to the program manager.

Radio stations may also have managers of sales/advertising, community relations, operations, and programming.

News Services

Most news services have one central office in Washington, D.C., where staff reporters and editors generate news stories for national distribution. A smaller number of news services have branch offices around the country, sometimes housing a single correspondent who covers the major news in the region.

The Associated Press is the largest news service in the United States. It's divided into "bureaus" (Boston, Detroit, Milwaukee, etc.). Smaller offices are called "correspondents."

Typically an AP bureau has a bureau chief, who's in charge. Under him are an assistant bureau chief and a news editor, who assigns stories to reporters. Larger bureaus may have business, sports, photo, and other editors who cover specific issue areas. A correspondent, who reports to the bureau chief, is in charge of smaller AP offices and may have reporters working under him or her.

The New York and Washington, D.C., offices of AP employ reporters and editors covering every type of national and international news you can think of. (For more on AP see Chapter 8, "Compile a Media List," and Chapter 30, "Make National News.")

Notes

Introduction

1. Stephen Engelberg, Jeff Gerth, and Katharine Q. Seelye, "Files Show How Gingrich Laid a Grand G.O.P. Plan," *New York Times*, December 3, 1995, p. A1.

Chapter Four

1. Carolyn Johnson,"Free Lemonade Comes with a Twist," *The Reporter: Citizens Coal Council Monthly Magazine*, Spring 1996, p. 6.
2. Jim Walsh, "Music with a Message," *St. Paul Pioneer Press*, February 24, 1996, p. 10E.
3. Alexander Cockburn, "Why I Love Bill Clinton," *The Nation*, June 16, 1997, p. 9.
4. Peter Montague, "Campaigning in the '90s," *Rachel's Environment and Health Weekly*, no. 480, February 8, 1996, p. 3.
5. See Lawrence Wallack, Lori Dorfman, David Jernigan, and Makani Themba, *Media Advocacy and Public Health* (Newbury Park, CA: Sage, 1993), p. 99.

Chapter Eight

1. National news outlets should be grouped into one "national market." On your list of national news outlets, make sure to include national outlets that have bureaus in your area. The *New York Times*, for example, might base one reporter in Dallas. Also on your national list, you should include photo editors who will consider your photos for publication and specialty publications, such as an industry newsletter, related to your cause.

Chapter Fifteen

1. Steven Durland, "Witness: The Guerilla Theater of Greenpeace," *High Performance,* no. 40, 1987, p. 33.

Chapter Thirty-Five

1. John Kessler, "Kessler Bids Adieu to His Readers," *Denver Post,* July 2, 1997, p. E1.

Index